THE ROYAL PSALMS

The
ROYAL
PSALMS

Keith R. Crim

JOHN KNOX PRESS
Richmond, Virginia

Library of Congress Catalog Card Number: 62-10237

BS
1445
.M H
C 74
1964

© M. E. Bratcher 1962

Printed in the United States of America

8075

To my father
who taught me
to love the Scriptures

Foreword

The first substantial contribution toward a satisfactory interpretation of the so-called Royal Psalms was made by Hermann Gunkel in his article on *Psalmen* published in *Die Religion in Geschichte und Gegenwart*, Vol. 4 (1st ed. 1913, 2nd ed. 1927). A popular treatment appeared in 1914 in *Preussische Jahrbücher*, 158, pp. 42-68, under the title "Die Königspsalmen." The most comprehensive study, however, was devoted to the subject in H. Gunkel and J. Begrich, *Einleitung in die Psalmen* (1933), pp. 140-171: it deals with virtually every phase of the subject from the Old Testament point of view. The Royal Psalms form a unity centering in the king about whose position in Israel we have a great deal of information in other writings of the Old Testament, though confined almost entirely to the situation pertaining in the Southern Kingdom. In these Psalms the ruler is referred to as the king, the son of the king, Yahweh's king, Yahweh's anointed, Yahweh's servant. He resides in Zion, Yahweh's city, and is a scion of David. His God is Yahweh and his people the children of Jacob or Yahweh's people. The duties performed by him were those which normally devolve upon the ruler of a people. All of these aspects of kingship demonstrate that the king was an actual native ruler.

All of these Psalms focusing upon royal activities connected with some phase in the life and experience of the king are closely associated with the cult. From various biblical and extrabiblical sources we know that celebrations of one sort or another were arranged by or for the king, doubtless to accentuate the splendor and glory of the kingdom. For example, there were royal feasts of various character such as the accession festivals, amply attested

7

by the accession Psalms, birthday celebrations, accession anniversaries, marriage occasions (Psalm 45), and certain religious observances such as the bringing of the ark to Jerusalem, the dedication of the Temple, commemoration of the royal house or sanctuary. In addition there were important occasions upon which services relevant thereto were held and in which the king played a significant role. When the king and his host went to war, there was a service invoking the divine blessing upon their enterprise. Upon their victorious return there was a thanksgiving celebration. In times of peril there were intercessions for deliverance; in times of illness in the royal family expiatory rites were conducted, and upon recovery thanksgiving services were held in gratitude for the favorable intervention of Yahweh. There were also royal funeral rites.

Gunkel calls attention to the fact that the pattern set forth in the preceding paragraph is just what might be expected because that is exactly the pattern current elsewhere in the ancient world, especially in Mesopotamia. There were accession festivals in both Assyria and Egypt. Royal celebrations marked the completion of palaces and canals; dedicatory rites marked the completion of a new residence or a royal arsenal. Feasts were also held in the palaces of conquered kings, presumably thanksgiving in nature honoring the deity for granting victory. Celebrations of similar nature took place after the return from a successful campaign against enemies. There were also memorial rites. As may be seen from a perusal of the relevant literary remains, all of these celebrations involved the king as ruler, representative of the god.

The Royal Psalms owe their composition to the requirements for the particular court festival to be celebrated. They were usually composed by the court musicians, though sometimes they were given by the king himself as in the case of David and Solomon. Such celebrations, whose main feature was the Psalm, were conducted either in the palace or in the sanctuary in the presence of the king and the court. It must be remembered that in these royal cultic functions it was the official musicians, and not the people, who rendered the hymns of praise to the king. That makes them court productions par excellence, for they voiced the official views and not those of outsiders, whether prophet or people. The varied character of the celebrations indicates that these psalms are not of the same type (Gattung), for they would be hymns of thanksgiving, lamentation, or some other type as the situation demanded. But all of them originally had to do with the reigning monarch and not with some future king, though later they doubtless came to have some eschatological significance. The fundamental importance of the Psalms in the cult has been demonstrated by Gunkel, and the cult, while possibly not a re-enactment of the original scene, as some scholars think, stressed the presence of God in the current situation as he was in that for which the given Psalm was composed.

Professor Sigmund Mowinckel of Oslo expanded Gunkel's thesis, adding twelve more Psalms to the category of Royal Psalms, together with 1 Samuel 2:1-10 and 2 Samuel 23:1-7. He had been greatly influenced by V. Grönbeck, the Danish anthropologist, whose studies of primitive societies led him to the belief that the king, occupying so important a place in Israel's faith and worship, must have been viewed as possessing the same divine qualities exhibited in other religions. He took his cue from the Babylonian *akitu* or New Year Festival. The rites connected with it re-enacted the struggle with and victory over chaos, and the king played a prominent role therein. At the beginning of the festival the king was divested of his official insignia; this act symbolized the reign of chaos. The Psalms belonging to that ritual present the king either as innocent or involved in the guilt of the whole nation. He was thus a mediator between the god and the people and hence was regarded as the savior of the people. Through his endurance and victory the nation received a new lease of life symbolized by the renewal of nature with its life-giving fruits. When that whole pattern was once transferred to a hypothetical Israelite New Year Festival, it is not difficult to see how the figure of the king assumed vast religious significance. Though Mowinckel argued so forcefully for the religious role of the king in Israel ("die ideale Inkorporation der Volksseele" and "als Inkarnation des nationalen Gottes"—*Psalmen-*

studien II, p. 301) and expanded the list of Royal Psalms, he never used these Psalms to any great extent to recover the New Year Festival in Israel. He makes a great deal of Psalm 132 in this connection (*Psalmenstudien* III, pp. 111-118; II, pp. 32-33) which he says is "the dramatic procession liturgy for a feast which repeats the first entrance of the ark, i.e., Yahweh, into Zion" and which presupposes the saga of the ark in 1 Samuel 4-6. Gunkel had already observed that we must probably think here of "an annual consecration festival" marking the founding of the Davidic dynasty (*Die Psalmen*, p. 568).

Subsequent studies by H. Schmidt, H. Gressmann, L. Dürr, E. R. Goodenough, A. Lods, C. R. North, H. Birkeland, J. Pedersen, J. Morgenstern, G. Widengren, I. Engnell, A. Bentzen, C. J. Gadd, H. Frankfort, H.-J. Kraus, and others* have done much to further our understanding of the subject both in its wider context and in its specific application in Israel. The most recent work is that of Professor A. R. Johnson entitled *Sacral Kingship in Ancient Israel* (Cardiff: University of Wales Press, 1955). It is a superb treatment of the whole theme on the basis of a careful study of the biblical texts bearing on the subject. He follows, in general, the broad outlines of Gunkel and Mowinckel but with more reserve than the latter because he interprets sacral kingship from within the Old Testament itself. For his interpretation he draws heavily upon the concept of corporate personality which he applies to the house of the king—the line of descent and the court—as the responsible ruling agent of Yahweh, an extension of the personality of Yahweh (p. 14). In line with such an interpretation of the *sacral kingship* it is easy to see the tremendously important place of the Royal Psalms in the religion of Israel. In their recitation in the cult they accentuate the continued interest

* As far back as 1893 D. G. Stevens, Jr., said of Psalms 110, 2, 45, 72, 22, 40, 16, 8, 69, generally regarded as Messianic Psalms, that they bear "witness to what the authors had in mind, and reveal the varying nature of the themes, in some cases purely secular, in others, matters concerning the fortunes of Israel, the Congregation of God." (*The Johns Hopkins University Circulars*, No. 106, June 1893, p. 108). Attention may be directed here to the important volume on *The Sacral Kingship: Contributions to the Central Theme of the VIIIth International Congress for the History of Religions*—Rome, April 1955 (Leiden: Brill, 1959). Section V (pp. 281-365) is devoted to the situation in Israel.

of Yahweh in his people through the king as the embodiment of his will and purpose. In a word, the cultic celebration became in itself the virtual assurance of the presence of Yahweh—as real and vital to the participants as the divine presence in the sacrament is to us.

Mr. Crim's book brings together the substance of a number of the above noted studies in such a way as to make us quite aware of the variety of trends in the detailed interpretation of the Royal Psalms together with their importance for the understanding of the king-messiah concept of H.-J. Kraus, *Die Königsherrschaft Gottes im Alten Testament* (Tübingen: J.C.B. Mohr, 1951) whose interpretation he follows in general. So far as the writer is aware this is the first attempt—apart from the chapters devoted to the Royal Psalms in A. Bentzen's *King and Messiah*, H. Ringgren's *The Messiah in the Old Testament*, S. Mowinckel's *He That Cometh*, and a few paragraphs in Samuel Terrien's *The Psalms and Their Meaning for Today*—at popular exposition of the subject in the English-speaking world. It is, therefore, an excellent introduction to this exceedingly significant though complex phase of Old Testament study whose perusal will prove most rewarding to diligent students of the Holy Scriptures.

Jacob M. Myers

Lutheran Theological Seminary
Gettysburg, Pennsylvania

Contents

		PAGE
KINGSHIP IN ANCIENT ISRAEL		15
I.	The Beginnings of the Monarchy	19
II.	David and Zion	29
III.	The Royal Zion Festival	40
IV.	Kingship and the Religion of Israel	52
V.	The Messiah	60
AN EXPOSITION OF THE ROYAL PSALMS		69
Psalm 2	The Coronation of God's Anointed	71
Psalm 18	The King's Salvation	76
Psalm 20	A Prayer for the King	85
Psalm 21	Blessings for the King	89
Psalm 45	A Royal Wedding	92
Psalm 72	The Nature of the King's Rule	97
Psalm 89	Lament for the House of David	101
Psalm 101	A Guide for Rulers	110
Psalm 110	King and Priest	113
Psalm 144	The Royal Welfare	118
2 Samuel 23:1-7	The Last Words of David	121
MESSIANIC PSALMS		125

Kingship in
Ancient Israel

Christians have always read and treasured the Old Testament because it tells of the promise of the Messiah. Since the church sees this promise fulfilled in Christ, anything that is an aid to understanding the Messianic hope is immediately relevant to the Christian faith. Not only so, but since this hope has traditionally been based on God's promises to David, it is involved in the whole question of the nature and significance of kingship in the Hebrew state. Another major reason for the perennial appeal of the Old Testament is the beauty and power of the Psalter, the most read and most treasured Old Testament book. These two areas of interest coincide in the question of the Royal Psalms. What do the Psalms tell us of the Messiah? This question touches on the central value of the Old Testament for the Christian church.

Over the past several decades, there has been great interest in the nature of kingship in ancient Israel and in the Psalms that deal with both human kingship and divine kingship. This interest has been a natural result of the increased knowledge of kingship in the ancient world and the study of the religious poetry of other ancient Near Eastern religions. One valuable contribution of this study has been the placing of biblical civilization in its proper historical context. Carried to an extreme, this can result in a view that the Bible is to be understood entirely in terms of the other religions that flourished in the same period. On the other hand, it can give a new appreciation of the uniqueness of the Bible to those whose eyes are open to differences as well as to similarities.

Much of the material, however, is not available in English, and much that has been written in English is highly technical in nature. The purpose of this book is to treat the biblical material that deals with Israelite kingship in such a way as to give the general reader who is familiar with the Bible an appreciation of the problems involved and an understanding of their importance for his interpretation of the Bible. In other words, it is hoped that this book will make these involved questions come alive for present-day students of the Bible who are not specialists in this field.

The study begins with an attempt to discover what type of kingship the Israelites had; and for this, the best sources are the historical books of the Old Testament. Since a discussion of other ancient types of monarchy would require another book, only general indications can be given of the ways in which Israelite royal ideology was unique.

The real significance of Israelite kingship lies in its theological basis. Anyone who would understand it must see how it is related to the theology of Israel and what role it played in the development of that theology. This opens up many possibilities for study and investigation.

It has always been known that certain phases of Israelite worship involved some dramatization. The Passover with its re-enactment of the events involved in the deliverance from Egypt illustrates this fact. In Christian worship, the sacraments of Baptism and the Lord's Supper, especially the latter, contain a certain amount of dramatization that differs in the various denominations but includes, at the very least, a re-enactment of certain events of religious significance. In the Psalms there are many hints that festivals not previously recognized as parts of

Israelite worship may have been celebrated during the period of the monarchy. These festivals appear to have been connected with the theology of kingship and to have been part of the agenda of the great autumn festival, the Feast of Tabernacles. The testimony of the historical books as well as the Psalter must be examined in order to evaluate this hypothesis.

Moreover, since kingship flourished at a critical time for Israelite religion and since its basic philosophy was thoroughly theological, the question arises whether or not the kingship may have had some profound effect on the religion of Israel. Was this influence on the whole constructive or destructive? What permanent theological contribution did the monarchy make?

At least a partial answer to the last question is found in the expectation of the Messiah, a future king of the line of David who would fulfill God's promises to David. This, however, raises other questions. When did the Messianic hope arise? What relation does it have to the royal ideology? What passages in the Old Testament, and particularly in the Psalms, can properly be interpreted as "Messianic"?

The treatment of such problems as these is a matter of great importance to every Christian. In the first place, an understanding of the nature and significance of the monarchy illuminates a large portion of the Old Testament, and anything that aids the understanding of the Bible is welcome. This understanding is vital to the general student as he reads the Bible and is confronted by the activity of God on behalf of his people. It is vital to the teacher and the preacher who seek to bring the truths of the Bible to those for whom they are responsible. Beyond this general significance, however, the subject is important because it deals with the hope for the coming of the Messiah—the hope that was fulfilled by the one "who was descended from David according to the flesh and designated Son of God in power according to the Spirit of holiness" (Romans 1:3-4, R.S.V.).

I

The Beginnings of the Monarchy

All Jerusalem was filled with excitement as the noise of shouting and the loud blasts of the ram's horn trumpets reached the city. King David was trying for the second time to bring the Ark of the Covenant into Jerusalem, his new capital city. The first attempt had come to a sudden stop when Uzzah, one of the priests in charge of the procession, put out his hand to steady the Ark and was struck dead on the spot. Quickly the king had the Ark put into the nearest house, that of a certain Obed-Edom, a Gittite, for fear that God would strike someone else dead that day. Then for three months the Ark stayed where it had been placed in the emergency, and its presence brought God's blessing to Obed-Edom.

When David heard that the Ark was again a source of blessing, he took courage and once more started out to move it to Jerusalem. When the procession had gone six paces, David sacrificed an ox and a fatling to prevent any further mishap. Then, wearing a linen ephod, a priestly garment, David danced before the Lord with all his might and led the procession as it made its way to the city. With the jubilant noise of shouts and trumpet blasts, the ark was at last carried into Jerusalem and placed carefully in the tent that had been prepared for it. Then David made further sacrifices—burnt offerings and peace offerings—and when they were finished, he blessed all the people in the name of Yahweh, the Lord. As an expression of the joyful mood that was felt by all, David had food for a celebration distributed to the people—loaves of bread, portions of meat, and a ration of raisins.

However, there was one discord that day. Michal, daughter of King Saul, sat at a window watching the procession. She had been David's wife when they were both young, but when David became an outlaw, her father had found her another husband. Only after Saul's death was David able to get her back and to be once again son-in-law to the first king of Israel. But the first love was gone. Too many changes had taken place in the nation and in the lives of these two. As Michal watched the procession of the Ark that day and thought how David was tightening his grip on her father's kingdom by bringing the symbol of God's presence into the city, bitterness welled up in her heart. Then David passed by, leaping and dancing, and evidently not as modestly clothed as is proper for religious processions today; and Michal despised him and compared him to the lewd men who had no shame in the sight of serving women. She told him as much when he came home. This marked the final estrangement of David and Michal as she taunted him with his behavior, and he answered with the sharp reminder that Yahweh had chosen him in preference to her father Saul and that he no longer needed to be allied to Saul's house by marriage in order to have a claim to the throne (2 Samuel 6).

David had finally broken with the family of Saul. He was now king over the two halves of the nation, Judah and Israel. He had won a new city in neutral territory between the two to be the capital. He had successfully laid claim to the traditions of the old tribal league of Israel by bringing to Jerusalem the league's central religious object, the Ark of the Covenant, the symbol of God's presence that unified the scattered and often feuding tribes. With his coronation the history of Israel and its religion had entered a new period. What was the meaning of this Davidic kingship?

The ancient centers of civilization in the Nile Valley and in the Tigris-Euphrates Valley had been ruled by kings for several thousand years before Israel became a nation. In those lands kingship was a part of the normal order of society; and without it, civilization, the favor of the gods, and the orderly course of the world of nature were inconceivable. It was not so in Israel, for the tribes were bound together by a covenant that God had made with them at Mt. Sinai; God himself was their king. The Israelites lived in the land of Canaan many generations before they had a human king.

It is a matter of dispute how old the concept of Yahweh as king really is. One indication can be found in the fact that the covenant at Sinai is very similar to the ancient suzerainty treaties known through the study of Hittite documents.[1] The Hittites with their capital in Asia Minor, the territory of the modern nation of Turkey, ruled one of the great empires of the ancient world in the centuries before the Israelites conquered Canaan. Their destruction was so complete that they were lost to history and survive chiefly in scattered references in the Old Testament. Uriah the Hittite, whom David had killed in order to get his wife, was a descendant of this once great empire. Only in the present century has archaeology unlocked the secrets of their civilization.

The Hittites ruled over many satellite states, and these subject nations were obliged to sign a treaty in which they gave up all right to have independent foreign relations with other countries, agreed to live peacefully with the other satellites, and promised to furnish troops for the wars of the Hittite emperor. These same features characterize the tribal league of Israel as formed in the covenant at Sinai.[2] The various Israelite tribes were united in the worship at the shrine which contained the Ark of the Covenant, the visible throne of the invisible God, their king. The tribes were obligated to live peacefully with each other, although they did not always do so, as the book of Judges makes clear. Significantly enough, the wars between the tribes were almost invariably the result of a breach of the covenant, and were thus attempts to enforce the provisions of the covenant. The individual tribes were not free to make alliances with other nations, with the Canaanite states, with Edom, or with Philistia, for instance. Also they were obligated to respond when there was a

[1] George E. Mendenhall, *Law and Covenant in Israel and the Ancient Near East*. Pittsburgh: The Biblical Colloquium, 1955.
[2] *Ibid.*

call to arms to fight some common enemy. In short, the tribes were bound together in loyalty to their divine king, Yahweh, whose presence was symbolized by the Ark of the Covenant, but they were free to go their own way in their internal affairs as long as they were loyal to the traditions of Sinai. This sort of league is commonly called an amphictyony by analogy to similar leagues of tribes in the ancient Greek world.[3]

During the first centuries after the settlement in Canaan this arrangement worked fairly well. In times of emergency God would send his Spirit into a chosen leader who then by mighty deeds defeated the enemies of the people and secured peace for the land. These leaders are, of course, the judges. Once the emergency was passed, the leader retired to private life or, in some cases, continued to exercise oversight over the affairs of the people. The office was not passed on from father to son but depended on free divine choice, the gift of the Spirit. As a result, this type of leadership is known as "charismatic"; that is, it depended on a "charisma," a Greek word meaning an outpouring of divine grace and strength. This word is the Greek original of the spiritual gifts bestowed on Timothy by the laying on of hands, 1 Timothy 4:14 and 2 Timothy 1:6.

In the period of the Judges there was one temptation to establish a hereditary monarchy. After Gideon had saved Israel from the ravages of the Midianites, the men of Israel offered him the kingship. "Rule over us," they said, "you and your descendants" (Judges 8:22). But Gideon refused both kingly honors for himself and the right to pass his office on to his descendants on the ground that Yahweh was the one who ruled over them. Although the idea was not attractive to Gideon, it appealed to one of his sons, Abimelech, who won the support of the city of Shechem and was king for a brief time. Before long, he alienated his supporters and in a spirit of vengeance destroyed Shechem and with it the basis of his kingship. In subsequent fighting, he was killed in the siege of the city of Thebez when a woman dropped a mill-

[3] John Bright, *A History of Israel*, ch 4. Philadelphia: The Westminster Press, 1959.

stone on his head. The brief episode of his kingdom is recorded in Judges 9.

The same chapter contains the well-known fable of Jotham, Abimelech's half brother. In that fable the trees wanted a king, but the olive tree, the fig tree, and the grape vine were unwilling to leave their fruitfulness to take up the unprofitable business of being king. Only the bramble was ready to be king. Not only was the bramble a worthless plant, but when dry, it was a dangerous cause of fire that could easily destroy the good trees (Judges 9:7-15). This gives a picture of the low esteem in which the Israelites held kingship in the period of the judges.

The circumstances changed greatly with the arrival of the Philistines in the coastal plain of Palestine. These sea peoples swept south out of the area of the Aegean Sea about the same time Israel invaded Canaan, and when they were unable to fight their way into Egypt they settled on the southern coast of Palestine. The earlier enemies of the tribal league had been a military threat from time to time. We read in the book of Judges of Moabites (chapter 3), Canaanites (4-5), Midianites (6-7), and Ammonites (11) who oppressed some of the tribes of Israel for a time and then were defeated by the judge whom God raised up for the purpose. These enemies were never able to act in a united manner for very long. But apparently the five Philistine cities, Gath, Gaza, Ashkelon, Ashdod, and Ekron, were joined together in a confederation. Each of them was under one-man rule. The word the Hebrew Bibles uses for these rulers, translated "lord" in the English versions, is not found in any other connection in the Bible. Although the details of the Philistine system are not clear, it was sufficiently strong to pose a constant menace to Israel. They also had chariots of war and new weapons made of iron and were able to maintain a monopoly over the manufacture of iron implements and thus keep the Israelites at a severe disadvantage. There was no blacksmith in Israel, so that even to sharpen a plowshare, a coulter, or an ax the Israelites had to go down to their arch enemies the Philistines (1 Samuel 13:19-20). How could the poorly armed Israelites resist weapons of iron? Even worse, they had no trained army and no permanent leadership. They had to wait for the Spirit to come on someone, who would then call the minutemen, the undisciplined militia, to come together and fight the well-equipped standing army of the Philistines. Even the Ark of the Covenant, the war palladium that had been present at such great victories and triumphs in the past, failed to bring victory and was captured by the enemy (1 Samuel 4).

To many it must have seemed that the end of the nation of Israel was at hand. It could be only a matter of time until they were absorbed by Philistia and the tribal league gone forever from the stage of history. But the national consciousness was strong, and the people were not ready to abandon hope. If the Philistines with their permanent rulers were strong, perhaps Israel needed something more permanent than occasional spiritual leadership. Perhaps a king could save Israel from her enemies.

It was an epoch-making step that the elders of Israel took when they went to see Samuel in Ramah and asked him to set up a king over the nation. Samuel's objections undoubtedly met with a sympathetic hearing from some of the elders, especially as they were reinforced by an oracle given Samuel by Yahweh. In this divine word it was made clear that the decision to have a king involved a rejection of the kingship of Yahweh similar to the idolatry Israel had practiced at various times after the Exodus from Egypt (1 Samuel 8:7-9). Samuel solemnly warned the elders that monarchy would produce a social revolution and overturn the simple economy of the land (1 Samuel 8:10-18).

Two conflicting views of the wisdom of setting up a king are reflected in the biblical material. First Samuel 9:1—10:16 gives a favorable account of the events surrounding the choice of Saul as king, and chapters 8 and 10:17-27 present the more hostile reaction.[4] Where such a momentous step was involved, it was inevitable that there would be conflicting views concerning its advisability, even in the mind of one man such as Samuel. No doubt others wavered too. But the issue had already been de-

[4] Bright (*ibid.*, pp. 166-167) regards these as two or possibly three parallel narratives.

cided by the Philistine threat. The nation had to change or perish.

What type of kingship was it that was chosen that day? The reason given by the elders for their action, "That we also may be like all the nations" (1 Samuel 8:20), has misled some into thinking the Israelites adopted the pattern of ancient kingship in which the king was considered to be divine and to bear the responsibility for the integration of society and nature. This integration was accomplished by religious observances that brought the activities of the people into harmony with the cycle of nature. In an agricultural society, this was especially important, for it was thought that above all the gods dealt with their people through natural phenomena.

This type of kingship existed in Egypt, and a similar type was to be found in Mesopotamia.[5] But it is not likely that such a system would have gained even the reluctant support of Samuel, for it was completely contrary to the covenant theology. Nor are the city-states of Canaan a likely place to look for the model of Israelite kingship. In almost all of these city-states kingship was dead or dying. However, among the small neighbor states on the east, Edom, Moab, and Ammon, there were two principles of kingship that seem to have been adopted or at least paralleled in Israel. The first of these is the principle of a national state following the boundaries of the people. This was different from the supra-national empires of Egypt, Assyria, and Babylon, and the later empire of David, which included many non-Israelites, and it was also different from the city-states of Canaan or the kingdom of Abimelech at Shechem. The kingdom of Saul was an Israelite national kingdom. Its boundaries were those of the Israelite people. The second principle is that of nondynastic rule. The old list of kings of Edom found in Genesis 36:31-39 gives kings who were not of the same family and who came from different parts of the country. This is evidently similar to the rule of the judges in Israel, although the Bible gives no hint as to how these Edomite kings were chosen.

[5] Henri Frankfort, *Kingship and the Gods.* Chicago: The University of Chicago Press, 1948.

An additional indication of the type of monarchy the Israelite elders had in mind is found in 1 Samuel 8:20. Following the indefinite and vague expression "be like all the nations," they gave two further reasons for the desirability of a king. First, they wanted a king to judge them, that is, to perform the duties that had belonged to the judges—administrative oversight of the affairs of the tribes and some responsibility for the religious life of the people. By so requesting, the elders were reiterating their objections to Samuel's efforts to pass his authority on to his worthless sons (1 Samuel 8:1-13). In the second place, they wanted a military leader, someone who would be able to lead the Israelite militia against the Philistines and other enemies. This would imply some type of permanent military force, if nothing more than a royal body guard, but the militia would continue to be the main fighting force of the nation. It is highly significant that nothing is said about any religious duties or privileges of the king similar to those involved in the monarchies of Egypt, Babylon, Assyria, and Canaan.

The choice of Saul is set forth at some length in 1 Samuel 9-10. Yahweh revealed to Samuel that Saul was the man chosen to be king, and in a private ceremony Samuel poured a vial of oil on Saul's head and kissed him. In this ceremony Samuel did not call Saul "king" but only "prince" (1 Samuel 10:1). The prophet then predicted a series of signs that were to be given to Saul, one of them being an outpouring of the Spirit. These all occurred shortly after Samuel and Saul parted, and through them Saul was clearly designated as a charismatic leader, that is, a ruler distinguished by his possession of the divine Spirit. Some time later the people gathered at Mizpah and there Saul was chosen by lot, presented to the people by Samuel, and hailed as king by the shout, "Long live the king!" (1 Samuel 10:24.) Perhaps "prince," the word used by Samuel, was a sacred term, and "king," the acclamation of the people, a more secular designation. It should be noted that Saul is called "prince" in the account favorable to his rule and "king" in the unfavorable one.

Opposition to Saul continued. Certain worthless fellows expressed their contempt of him, but he ignored their remarks. Very soon, however, an opportunity arose for Saul to silence them by his success as a leader of the people. The Ammonites besieged Jabesh-Gilead, an Israelite city in the area east of the Jordan River. When word of this siege reached Saul, he was filled with the Spirit and mustered three hundred thousand of the men of Israel and thirty thousand from Judah. Swiftly leading his men across the Jordan, he relieved the siege and thoroughly defeated the Ammonites. In his hour of triumph, he graciously spared the lives of those who had opposed his kingship, and Israel seemed to be on the road to a new era of greatness (1 Samuel 11:1-11).

According to the Hebrew text of 1 Samuel 13:1, Saul reigned over Israel for only two years. It is difficult, if not impossible, to fit so many events into such a short period, but in any case his kingdom did not last long. The biblical account gives two separate incidents as the basis for God's rejection of Saul. In 1 Samuel 13:1-15 is found the account of the action at Gilgal. Saul's son Jonathan opened the war of liberation from Philistine rule by wiping out a garrison of the Philistines at Geba. This was a signal to the Philistines that trouble was coming, and they responded by sending a large army, including chariots, to put down the insurrection. Saul summoned the Israelite militia to Gilgal near Jericho and waited for Samuel to come to make a sacrifice and secure God's help for the war. Gilgal was the first place west of the Jordan where the Israelites under Joshua encamped and was undoubtedly long considered an especially sacred spot (Joshua 5:9-10). Samuel, however, was in no hurry to go to Gilgal. Each day saw Israelite morale sink lower, and many of those who had come out in a burst of patriotism now slipped silently away and hid in caves, or thickets, or pits. Saul saw his army melting away, and still Samuel did not come. Finally, in desperation, Saul offered the burnt offering himself, but he had no sooner finished than Samuel arrived. On learning what Saul had done, Samuel upbraided him and announced that Yahweh had rejected Saul as king and had sought out someone else, a "man after his own heart" (1 Samuel 13:14).

The other incident is recorded in 1 Samuel 15. Saul failed to complete the destruction of Amalek as required by the concept of a holy war in which no spoil was to be taken; everything was to be devoted to Yahweh by being destroyed. Like the initiative Saul took in offering sacrifice, this was also an offense in the realm of religion. Certainly the kingship of Saul did not follow any pattern of divine kingship; on the contrary, the king was rebuffed at every attempt he made to exercise religious functions. After this, Yahweh withdrew the gift of the Spirit (1 Samuel 16:14), and the very basis of Saul's kingship was destroyed. From then on, it was merely a matter of time until Saul's kingdom met its end. The stage was set for a new form of state which, although founded on the direct gift of God's Spirit, soon grew far beyond the ideas of government previously accepted in Israel. A dynasty arose that was to last as long as the kingdom did and was to influence greatly the religion of Israel.

II

David and Zion

An indication of the importance of David's career for the nation Israel can be found in the fullness of the biblical material that deals with his exploits. Old Testament history is quite different from histories written in modern times, and the ancient documents are often silent where we wish they would speak. But when the history of David is compared with that of Saul or Solomon or any of the other kings found in the Bible, it is at once clear that the relative completeness of the record must have been prompted by a special interest in his life and work. A careful study of the changes instituted by David and their permanent effect on the culture and religion of Israel shows that this unusual attention is quite justified.

David has always been pictured as a heroic figure. Children in Sunday school learn of his fight with Goliath and his bravery as a shepherd defending his father's flocks against wild animals. This side of his character and his career as a military man are essential to an understanding of his impact on history. He was at first a member of Saul's permanent band of soldiers, and when the king's jealousy forced him to flee for his life, he became the head of his own band of freebooters waging guerrilla warfare in the Judean wilderness (1 Samuel 18-26). Eventually he moved into the territory of Israel's enemies, the Philistines, and hired himself and his men to Achish, king of Gath, as mercenary troops (1 Samuel 27:1-7). In return for his services, he received the city of Ziklag as a fief, and using that as a base, he launched raids on the Amalekites and other traditional enemies of Israel. He played a double game in this, using the spoil to buy friends among the inhabitants of the Judean hill country while telling his liege lord, Achish, that he had been raiding the nearby Judean settlements (1 Samuel 30:26-31). Achish was thus deceived into believing that David was making himself hateful to his own countrymen and making it impossible for him ever to be received among them again. Because the other Philistine lords suspected his loyalty, however, he was not required to fight against Saul and the Israelite militia in the battle of Mt. Gilboa where Saul lost his life and the militia was scattered.

This interlude served David's career in three ways. First, and most obviously, he was able to save his life and survive these critical times. He was safe from both Saul and the Philistines. Second, he won friends among the Judeans. Since they were his kinfolk, they would naturally be disposed to support him in preference to a member of the house of Saul, but it is unlikely that the spoils he distributed failed to strengthen his position. In the third place, he built up a well-disciplined body of professional soldiers who were loyal to him rather than to a city or state and who could be counted on to further his ambitions. This elite guard helped him to power, kept him in power, and enabled him to pass the kingdom on to the heir of his choice.

The main unit of David's mercenaries was usually referred to as the "Cherethites and Pelethites"; that is, they were recruited from among the Philistines and other Aegean peoples (2 Samuel 8:18; 20:23; 1 Kings 1:38-44). In 2 Samuel 20:7 they appear along with two other groups, namely "Joab's men" and "all the mighty men." Joab, as anyone familiar with the biblical material knows, played a rather dubious role as David's lieutenant, but in spite of his excesses David apparently needed him and was unwilling to get rid of him, although after the death of Absalom he made an attempt to give Joab's job as commander of the militia to Amasa. Joab solved this threat to his position by murdering Amasa (2 Samuel 20:4-10, 23). Another military unit at David's disposal was that of Ittai the Gittite and his men. "Gittite" designates him as a "man of Gath" and thus another non-Israelite (2 Samuel 15:18f.). Perhaps he became acquainted with

David when the latter was in the service of the king of Gath. The "king's servants" seems to have been a general designation for these various units under David's personal command and bound in loyalty to him and his house rather than to the nation. The extremely great importance of David's personal bodyguard for the successful execution of his policies is illustrated not only by their loyalty to him when the militia defected in the revolts of Absalom and Sheba (2 Samuel 15-20) but also in the role played by the Cherethites and Pelethites at Solomon's coronation in making his throne secure (1 Kings 1:38-44).

After the death of Saul the way was open for David to return from exile and make his bid for power, although he was still a vassal of the Philistines. It is probable that he had the consent of his overlords for the action he now took. He chose Hebron, a city that was centrally located with respect to the southern components of the ancient tribal league and that had the further advantage of being located in the territory where his own kinsmen lived. Second Samuel 2:4 records how the men of Judah came to Hebron and anointed David king, possibly at the ancient sacred site of the Oaks of Mamre. This, however, was only one step toward the goal. After the failure of Saul, there may well have been an upsurge of the old popular feeling against kings. In any case, Saul's general, Abner, had fled to Transjordania and put one of Saul's sons, Eshbaal, on the throne of Israel.[1] This kingship seems to have had little popular support, and Eshbaal was clearly not a charismatic leader. His rule lasted only a brief time and was not a serious obstacle in David's path. It served, however, to widen the rift between North and South.

Second Samuel 3 and 4 record the bloodshed and the treachery that marked the end of Eshbaal's rule. David managed not only to remain innocent of the blood of Abner and Eshbaal but also

---

[1] In 2 Samuel he is called Ish-bosheth "man of shame." This is clearly a pejorative name used to avoid the objectionable Ishbaal (or Eshbaal) found in 1 Chronicles 9:40. William Foxwell Albright holds that Esh-Baal means "Baal exists," rather than the usual translation "Man of Baal." *Archaeology and the Religion of Israel*, p. 113. Baltimore: The Johns Hopkins Press, 1946.

to convince the people of his innocence. This required political skill added to moral rectitude.

David's power increased rapidly. The men of Israel came to David in Hebron and offered him their loyalty. They acknowledged his service to the state in the days of Saul and the fact that Yahweh had chosen him to be a prince and a shepherd over Israel. At Hebron David made a covenant with them, and they anointed him king over Israel (2 Samuel 5:1-3). Seemingly, he now held the dual office, King of Judah and King of Israel.

Up until this time the Philistines had not interfered with David, for they still regarded him as their vassal and welcomed his kingship over Judah as a means of dividing and ruling their subject territory. But when the Israelite leaders came to Hebron and made David their king, the Philistines thought matters had gone too far. They promptly mustered their forces and moved into the valley of Rephaim west of Jerusalem, evidently in an attempt to cut Israel off from Judah. David defeated them decisively, but they quickly returned with what must have been the strongest force they could muster, for their supremacy in Palestine was threatened. Once again they were beaten, and David pursued them back to their own territory, ending for good their threat to Israel (2 Samuel 5:17-25).

David was now the master of Palestine and was free to proceed with both the construction of his government and the expansion of his empire. In order to consolidate his position, however, he needed to avoid arousing the jealousy of either of the two kingdoms over which he ruled. With this end in view, he captured the ancient Jebusite stronghold of Jerusalem which lay in neutral territory between Israel and Judah and had never belonged to either. In taking this step, David moved slowly and carefully. Although the kingdom of Eshbaal lasted only one or two years, David reigned in Hebron for seven and a half years according to 2 Samuel 2:11. In this as in his other ventures, David was able to wait until the time was ripe for action. In 2 Samuel 5:6 it is recorded that the king and his men, that is to say, David and his professional soldiers, captured the city without any help from the Israelite or Judean militia and called it the city of David.

It may well be that David incorporated Jerusalem into neither of his two kingdoms but ruled it as a city-state—he himself being its king and the legitimate successor of the Jebusite monarchs by right of conquest.[2] On this view, the inhabitants remained unmolested, and only David with his court and his professional troops moved there. This is probably correct since the Bible does not mention any deportation or execution of the population, but the question of David's being the legitimate successor of the Jebusite kings is one that cannot be decided conclusively.

There is no evidence that there was a Jebusite king ruling in Jerusalem at this period. None is mentioned in 2 Samuel 5, and the fact that the inhabitants spoke tauntingly to David implies a council of elders as the supreme authority. To be sure, Joshua 10:1-27 records how Adoni-zedek, king of Jerusalem, allied himself with four other kings of city-states and fought against the Israelites, but roughly two centuries had passed since that time, and it is quite possible that by David's day monarchy had been replaced by oligarchy in Jebusite Jerusalem.

These are the primary political and military factors in the rise of David. His subsequent conquests and the expansion of his empire show the development of these factors but add nothing new. He was a military commander of outstanding ability at the head of an elite army of professional soldiers completely loyal to him. He had avoided the guilt of destroying the house of his rival Saul and had been anointed king by the two parts of the nation. He ruled in the city of Jerusalem, his personal possession by right of conquest, and by virtue of this neutral position he avoided the jealousy of Israel and Judah and the danger of domination by either. It is easy to see that his rule was the antithesis of any "divine kingship." Here was no institution with its roots in primeval time; it was a product of the tenth century B.C. Here is no order essential to the existence of society; Israelite society had existed for several centuries before the appearance of this monarchy.

This is not to say that Israelite kingship was purely secular in

[2] Martin Noth, *The History of Israel*, p. 190. New York: Harper & Brothers, 1958.

nature. The religious sanctions for and the sacral nature of
David's office were of the utmost importance. To begin with,
he was a charismatic leader in that he had been anointed by the
prophet Samuel and designated leader by the presence of the
Spirit. In addition, David's moving the Ark of the Covenant to
Jerusalem marked his city as the religious center of the nation
and the inheritor of the traditions of the old tribal league of the
days of the judges. In the third place, an oracle of Yahweh
through Nathan the prophet promised David that his sons would
sit on his throne forever. This Davidic covenant was of the
greatest importance for the subsequent history of the nation and
for the development of doctrine. Finally, David exercised certain
sacral functions. He was not a priest-king, but he assumed a large
measure of responsibility for the cult. These matters require con-
sideration in some detail.

In the stories of David's rise to power, it is clearly pointed out
that he was a charismatic leader. After Yahweh's rejection of
Saul, Samuel received a divine command to go to the house of
Jesse the Bethlehemite and secretly anoint one of his sons king.
David was designated as the one chosen, and when Samuel
anointed him the Spirit of Yahweh came mightily upon him and
stayed with him from then on (1 Samuel 16:13). He was thus set
apart from ordinary men as the "Anointed of Yahweh." The accounts of David's relation to Saul illustrate the fact that now
David and not Saul was the one favored of the Lord. This was
of great importance for the monarchy. Saul's office was based
on the presence of God's Spirit with him, and if the Spirit had
passed from him to someone else, all claim Saul had to the kingdom had passed with it. This is the key to understanding Saul's
reaction to the song of the women who greeted the army return-
ing from battle with the Philistines:

> "Saul has slain his thousands,
> And David his ten thousands."
> (1 Samuel 18:7.)

Saul's anger was not so much the result of jealousy and spite as it
was the expression of his foreboding that David would wrest the

kingdom from him. "What more can he have but the kingdom?"
(1 Samuel 18:8.)

When David was made king over Judah and over Israel, there
was no indication of a fresh outpouring of the Spirit, but a recog-
nition of David's charismatic character is implied, particularly in
the words of the Israelite leaders when they acknowledged Yahweh's choice of David as "Shepherd" and "Prince" (2 Samuel
5:1-2). It should be noted that in addition to the anointing by
Samuel, David was anointed twice more, first as king of Judah
(2 Samuel 2:4) and then as king of Israel (2 Samuel 5:3). With
respect to the divine choice and the bestowal of spiritual gifts,
David was in the old tradition of the judges and King Saul.

In Chapter I the manner in which the Ark of the Covenant
was brought to Jerusalem has been described. The importance
of the Ark in the past made this a significant step. Dating from
the period when Israel wandered in the wilderness, the Ark
had served as the central cultic object of the tribal league after
the settlement in Canaan. The tribes lived in isolation from one
another but were bound together by loyalty to a central shrine,
the site of the Ark.

The Ark was at Shiloh for a time (1 Samuel 4), but in the
course of the wars with the Philistines the Israelites decided to
revive the old use of the Ark as a war palladium and took it into
battle against the Philistines. When God did not honor this use
of the Ark, Israel was defeated and the Ark fell into the hands
of the Philistines. Shiloh was destroyed at this time, for nothing more is heard of it as a sanctuary except for Jeremiah's
comments on its destruction (Jeremiah 7:12-14). The Ark merely
brought curses on the Philistines, and they sent it back to Israelite territory to the town of Beth-shemesh (1 Samuel 6). From
there it was sent on to Kiriath-jearim (1 Samuel 7:1-2), where
it remained until the time of David. It should not be considered
improbable for the Ark to survive all these vicissitudes. It was
regarded with awe by both Israelites and Philistines and would
undoubtedly be accorded the same careful treatment by both.

David moved this sacred object to Jerusalem, and by so doing
he accomplished at least two purposes. He made Jerusalem the

cultic center of the nation, thus vividly demonstrating the divine approval of his political measures for the unification of the country, and he laid claim to being the legitimate successor of the amphictyonic league with all its sacral traditions. It may also be that he wanted to use the Ark as a war palladium again, for in his report of the siege of Rabbah in Ammon, Uriah stated that the Ark and Israel and Judah were abiding in tents or booths (2 Samuel 11:11). This would indicate that the Ark had been taken into battle. After the time of David, there is no indication that the Ark was again used in this manner.

In the chapter that follows immediately on the account of David's bringing the Ark to Jerusalem (2 Samuel 6), is the passage that first records God's promise to David that his sons would sit on the throne after him, that David would be permitted to bequeath his "charisma" to his posterity (2 Samuel 7:1-17).

David had completed his cedar palace and conquered his foes on every side. He then considered the contrast between his own palace and the tent where the Ark of Yahweh was kept and told the Prophet Nathan of his desire to erect a more suitable sanctuary for the central cultic object of the Israelite tribal league. Nathan at first gave his approval, but that night in a vision he heard the word of God rejecting David's proposal. In all the time since the Exodus, God had dwelt in the sacred tent, and he had not commanded any of the judges[3] to replace this nomadic shrine with one more conformable to the usage of Canaan. David himself had been taken from the pasture, where he tended sheep as had his nomadic ancestors, and made a *nagid*, a prince over God's people. God not only gave him victory over all his enemies on every hand but also bestowed on him a name like the names of the mighty ones of the earth. God's people Israel also are established and given rest from warfare. Then we have the great contrast between man's intention and God's. David thought he would build a house for God, but God will establish a house, a dynasty, for David. After David's death, his own son shall sit on the throne and God will establish that

[3] Thus 1 Chronicles 17:6. Second Samuel 7:7 reads "tribes" in the Hebrew, a copyist's error.

throne forever. Moreover, God will be the father of the coming king, and the king God's son. But this is a father-son relationship quite different from that between David and the promised king, who is David's "seed" and proceeds out of David's loins. That is to say, the coming king is God's son by adoption. The king will stand under the constant judgment of God; if he commits iniquity, God will chasten him with the rod of men and the stripes of the children of men, not beyond that which a human being can stand. Moreover, this punishment will not extend to God's breaking the covenant which he has made with David. God will not discontinue his covenant love with David's line, but will make the throne of David secure forever.

What are the significant elements of this oracle? 1. God promises to David a successor on the throne; 2. The successor will be the physical descendant of David; 3. He will be the adopted son of God; 4. The dynasty will continue to rule and the throne be secure forever; 5. The king is liable to error and consequent divine chastisement; 6. The accomplishment of these promises is dependent on the initiative of God himself. A firm theological basis has been laid not only for David's own kingship but for a radical departure from traditional Israelite political principles. Dynastic rule was replacing charismatic rule.

The last point to be dealt with is David's exercise of sacral functions. Sacral kingship is not the same as divine kingship. To be sure the term sacral can be used concerning the office of the Pharaohs of Egypt, who were considered divine, but in itself it merely indicates that the king had a certain relation to the religious life of his nation. That relation must then be defined on the basis of the historical evidence. In the case of Israel, the definition must come primarily from the biblical material and not from an arbitrary pattern derived from other cultures.

The occasion on which Saul offered sacrifice has been referred to in the preceding chapter. Saul met opposition even to his claim to emergency powers in sacral matters, but the fact that he endeavored to exercise a priestly function indicates that he had a wider view of the royal office than Samuel did.

In the following period, when David was king, it is recorded that he offered sacrifice on two separate occasions. The first of these is the removal of the Ark of the Covenant to Jerusalem (2 Samuel 6:17-18), and the second is the sacrifice on the threshing floor of Araunah the Jebusite after David's sin in numbering the people (2 Samuel 24:25). In neither of these incidents is there any indication in the text that David did wrong in offering sacrifice. The parallels in 1 Chronicles reinforce this fact. To be sure, in the account of bringing up the Ark, the Chronicler mentions priests and Levites and implies that Levites offered the sacrifices (1 Chronicles 15:26-27), but in the story of the sacrifice at the threshing floor it is clear that David himself made the sacrifice and was rewarded with divine fire from heaven to consume it (1 Chronicles 21:26). In other words, the Deuteronomic histories gave their tacit approval to David's offering sacrifice and even the Chronicler did not disapprove. Both histories record David's wearing a linen ephod (2 Samuel 6:14, 1 Chronicles 15:27) and his dancing in the ceremony, and these, too, are clearly sacral functions.

Solomon continued this tradition and sacrificed and burnt incense in the high places, in particular the great high place at Gibeon, where he offered a thousand burnt offerings and was rewarded by a dream vision of Yahweh and God's manifest approval (1 Kings 3:3-5). At the dedication of the Temple he offered peace offerings, and in addition, in the middle court of the Temple he offered burnt offerings, meal offerings, and the fat of the peace offerings (1 Kings 8:62-64). Not only this, but three times annually he offered burnt offerings and peace offerings on the altar he had built for Yahweh, and also burnt incense (1 Kings 9:25). It is worthy of note that along with the offering of sacrifice Solomon also blessed the people and offered prayer before the altar (1 Kings 8:54ff.). His right to act in this way was not questioned any more than that of his father had been.

In 2 Chronicles a conflict between king and priest is recorded in explanation of the bare statement in 2 Kings 15:5 that king Uzziah was a leper. Second Chronicles 26:16-21 tells how the king's heart was proud, and he went into the Temple to burn incense on the altar. There he was confronted by Azariah the

priest and eighty other priests who claimed the right of sacrifice as pertaining solely to the descendants of Aaron. When
Uzziah angrily resisted, he broke out with leprosy and was
thrust out of the sanctuary. Thus, by the time Chronicles was
written in the postexilic period, this sacral function of the king
was categorically rejected, but even then there was no attempt
to dispute the accepted fact that Solomon and David had themselves offered sacrifice.

As the biblical record gives no information on the subject,
the origin of the royal prerogative of sacrifice in Israel must
remain obscure. Most probably, however, it was derived from
other nations where offering sacrifice was a part of the work of
a king. In the course of time, such a function would come more
and more to be delegated to subordinates, and in Israel it was
eventually denied to the king altogether.

In the early period of the monarchy the king exercised con-
siderable authority over the priests, even though the priesthood
existed independently of any royal authority. Solomon took the
drastic step of deposing the priest Abiathar who had been his
father's companion in the days before David came to the throne
and who had served as priest together with Zadok throughout
the reign of David. Abiathar made the mistake of supporting
Solomon's rival to the throne, Adonijah, and on this ground he
was banished to his native town of Anathoth (1 Kings 1:7; 2:26-
27). In an enumeration of officials it is stated, moreover, that
David's sons were priests (2 Samuel 8:18). The information is
too meager to allow the drawing of detailed conclusions, but at
the very least it indicates a royal power over the priestly office.

The activity of David in the religious realm and the influence
of theology on the history of his kingdom are certainly sufficient
to justify designating his kingship as sacral. The significant fact
is that this new institution became so assimilated by normative
Israelite religion as it had come down from the past that it both
conserved the positive values in the traditions of the tribal
league and gave them new life and vitality. Jerusalem and the
Davidic dynasty became not a threat to Yahwism but rallying
points in its war with the pagan world.

III

The Royal Zion Festival

The theory that lies behind an institution is often most clearly seen in the ceremonials connected with it. At his ordination a minister of the gospel takes vows that are determined by the nature of the denomination to which he belongs. A young couple being joined in marriage promise to live together according to the laws of God and the state. The president of the United States in his inauguration swears to uphold the Constitution. So, too, in ancient Israel the monarchy stands revealed in the ceremonies of kingship. The ceremony that first springs to mind is the coronation of a new king, and the two biblical accounts of coronations are highly instructive. But this was probably not the only significant royal festival. Recent scholarship has explored the possibility that each year on the opening day of the autumn festival, the Feast of Tabernacles, the Israelites—and the Judeans after the division of the monarchy—celebrated the establishment of the Davidic dynasty and the divine choice of Jerusalem.[1]

Very little material is available for a reconstruction of the coronation ritual of the Judean kings. Indeed, even a partial description is preserved in connection with only two kings, Solomon and Joash, both of whom were crowned under rather unusual circumstances. First, let us consider the coronation of Solomon as recorded in 1 Kings 1:32-48. Solomon was the first king in Israel to receive the throne from his father, and thus his is the first regular coronation. In order to forestall the seizure of the throne by Adonijah, David had Solomon installed as co-

[1] This theory was very ably presented by the German scholar Hans-Joachim Kraus, *Die Königsherrschaft Gottes im Alten Testament.* Tübingen: J.C.B. Mohr, 1951.

regent, and in this way Solomon was able to establish his right to inherit his father's throne. In view of the fact that the two parts of the Israelite nation had been united only in their allegiance to David, while the other tribes and peoples in the empire were included because they had been conquered by David, it is doubtful that the throne of so complex a political entity as the vast empire of David could have retained its power if the succession had been decided by means other than inheritance.

David commanded that Solomon should ride on the royal mule and go in the company that included Zadok the priest and Nathan the prophet to the pool Gihon, just outside the city to the east. The text gives no indication as to why Gihon was chosen, but it perhaps had some connection with the ceremonial of the old Jebusite kings of Jerusalem. Certainly there was no Israelite precedent for a coronation there with the possible exception of David's becoming king of Jerusalem. With the horn of oil from the sacred tent where the Ark was kept (vs. 39), Zadok the priest anointed Solomon, signifying Yahweh's choice of him as king. Then, after the trumpet blast, the people acclaimed him with piping and great joy and with the shout "May the king live!" What followed is obscure, but evidently there was a procession to the royal palace and a formal seating of the new king on the throne. In the report to Adonijah (vs. 46), it is stated that Solomon was sitting on the throne of the kingdom, so probably some enthronement ceremony is to be postulated. The presence of the mercenary troops of King David, the Cherethites and Pelethites, while of no apparent religious significance, illustrates the military basis of Solomon's kingship.

The account of the coronation of Joash in 2 Kings 11 is somewhat more precise, but it is still far from being a complete program of the event. On the face of the matter, it is likely that certain changes will have occurred in the century and a half since Solomon's accession to power. Athaliah, mother of king Ahaziah, on hearing of the death of her son, had seized power and tried to wipe out the Davidic line; but one royal son, the infant Joash, was saved by his aunt Jehosheba, who hid him in

the Temple. When the time seemed ripe, Jehoida the priest secured the support of the Temple guards and staged a coup d'etat
that put the young boy on the throne (2 Kings 11:1-21). There
is no mention of a ceremony at Gihon, and all the events seem
to have taken place in the Temple. The central shrine of Israel
had replaced the Canaanite sacred spring. Nor is there any
reference to a royal mule, perhaps because the requirements of
secrecy precluded these features. Within the Temple there was a
particular place for the king to stand, "by the pillar" or "on the
platform" (vs. 14). It has been suggested that this may be the
podium of Solomon mentioned in 2 Chronicles 6:13.[2] The king's
standing there for the ceremony was according to the regula-
tions for the occasion (vs. 14), and this fact seems to have im-
pressed Athaliah profoundly when she saw it. Then the crown
was placed on the young king's head, and he was given the
"testimonies." This term has called forth much speculation.
Most commentators propose emending the word to read "bracelets" after the parallel phrase in 2 Samuel 1:10 where the crown
and bracelets of the dead Saul were brought to David. This
proposal is unnecessary. The word "testimony" is best understood by comparison with the word "decree" which is often
parallel to it in the Bible.[3] In Psalm 2:7 "decree" refers to the
verbal evidence of divine sonship—most probably the oracle of
the Davidic Covenant as recorded in 2 Samuel 7. Whether this
was already in documentary form when Psalm 2 was written
we cannot be sure, but it had undoubtedly been written down
by the time of Joash. Now, in Psalm 2 there is no explicit mention of the word "covenant," but in Psalm 89:39 "covenant" and
"crown" are brought together, and this latter is a Royal Psalm
dealing specifically with the matter of God's covenant with
David. Some additional evidence is contained in Psalm 105:10
where "decree" (the A.S.V. reads "statute") and "covenant" are
in parallelism. Since Psalm 2 gives the content of the "testimony"
in verses 7-9, it is even possible that this Psalm was recited on

[2] Gerhard von Rad, "Das Judäische Königsritual," *Theologische Litera-
turzeitung*, pp. 211-216, 1947.
[3] This view follows the suggestion of von Rad. *Ibid.*, p. 37.

the occasion of Joash's coronation. In any case, there is no need to emend the wording of 2 Kings 11:12.

To return to Joash's crowning, it is recorded that they made him king and anointed him, undoubtedly with the sacred oil reserved for such occasions. Then followed the acclamation of the people as they clapped their hands and shouted, "May the king live!" (2 Kings 11:12.) Later it is mentioned that the new monarch "sat on the throne of the kings" (2 Kings 11:19).

A comparison of these two ceremonies thus reveals that although there were differences brought about by the passage of time and the different circumstances of each coronation they are in their essentials identical. The ceremony took place in a holy spot, at the sacral pool and spring of Gihon, or in the Temple; the king was anointed by the priest and acclaimed by the people, following which he sat on the throne. The incomplete nature of the accounts is sufficient warning against drawing far-reaching conclusions from the omissions from one account or the other. It should be noted also that the two elements of charismatic rule—first, choice by the deity, now formalized as anointing by a priest, and second, acclamation by the people—were preserved even within the ritual of the dynasty and its hereditary kingship. The charismatic principle had been applied to an entire dynasty by virtue of the covenant with its founder.

The idea of a festival of kingship at the autumn feast has a long history. It was suggested by the discovery of somewhat similar festivals in the ancient world, the "Sed Festival" for the renewal of kingship in Egypt[4] and the Mesopotamian New Year Festival.[5] The theory that each year on the first day of the Feast of Tabernacles a celebration of the Enthronement of Yahweh took place was popularized by the Norwegian scholar Sigmund Mowinckel and gained wide acceptance.[6] Starting with the so-called "Enthronement Psalms," 47, 93, 95, 97, and 99, he included others that had some elements in common with these until he had designated sixty-seven of the Psalms as belonging

[4] Frankfort, *Kingship and the Gods*, pp. 79-88.
[5] *Ibid.*, pp. 331-333.
[6] Sigmund Mowinckel, *Psalmenstudien II*. Oslo: Jacob Dybwad, 1922.

to this hypothetical festival. The nature of Israelite religion and the biblical data seem to be more consonant with the theory of a Royal Zion Festival, however, and we shall first consider this theory and then attempt to deal with the "Enthronement Psalms."[7]

We have already seen that 2 Samuel 6 records how David brought the Ark of the Covenant to Jerusalem and in so doing made the city of Zion the successor to the old cultic centers of the tribal league. The following chapter, 2 Samuel 7, gives the oracle of Nathan to David in which are proclaimed God's choice of David and the promise that David's house will continue to rule over the nation. The importance of these events for the history of the monarchy and the continuance of the Davidic dynasty has been stressed above in Chapter II, but no effort was made to consider how this message was communicated to the people. H.-J. Kraus has advanced the view that the choice of Jerusalem and the Davidic dynasty was celebrated on the first day of the Feast of Tabernacles in what he called a "Royal Zion Festival."[8]

In support of this theory, Kraus produced two types of evidence: one, the indications in the historical books that such a feast was celebrated, and two, the portions of the Psalter that appear to be the cultic songs for the feast; that is, the hymns that were used as a part of the festival.[9]

For the first point, he began with the two chapters that give the account of the bringing of the Ark to Jerusalem and the justification for this step, that is, 2 Samuel 6 and 7; he then inquired how David's action here was justified to the people. Surely many non-Judeans who went to Jerusalem for the Feast of Tabernacles must have questioned this new state of affairs, this departure from ancient usage. If the bringing of the Ark

[7] In my unpublished dissertation, *Israelite Kingship and the Royal Psalms* (Union Theological Seminary in Virginia, 1959) I have endeavored to evaluate Mowinckel's theories in the light of recent scholarship and have concluded that there was no festival of the enthronement of Yahweh in ancient Israel. See Hans-Joachim Kraus, *Psalmen* Vol. I, pp. 197-205, Neukirchen, Kreis Moers: Buchhandlung des Erziehungsvereins, 1960.

[8] Kraus, *Die Königsherrschaft Gottes,* p. 48.

[9] *Ibid.,* pp. 30-40, 50-90.

into Jerusalem by David was repeatedly re-enacted and the prophetic word that empowered David to do this was solemnly proclaimed, the divine basis of the Davidic dynasty and its rule in Jerusalem would soon become accepted by the people.

Is there any evidence to support this? Let us look first at the historical books. Solomon's dedication of the Temple is recorded in 1 Kings 8. It took place significantly enough at the great feast in the seventh month, that is the autumn festival, the Feast of Tabernacles (1 Kings 8:2). This certainly was not accidental. The construction of the Temple had taken seven years and was finally completed in the eighth month according to 1 Kings 6:38. Evidently Solomon waited almost an entire year before the dedication at the great festival. The procession of the Ark that took place when David brought it up to Jerusalem was repeated and this sacred cult object installed in the new sanctuary. It is quite possible that this was not a unique occurrence but was repeated annually; that is, the "Royal Zion Festival" was regularly celebrated on the first day of the Feast of Tabernacles, the old festival of the tribal covenant.

After the division of the kingdom, Jeroboam organized a festival in competition to the Judean feast and held it on the fifteenth day of the eighth month "like unto the feast that is in Judah, and he offered upon the altar" (1 Kings 12:32-33, K.J.V.). The question must be asked, like what feast? Since Jeroboam's feast was an annual affair, it could not be an imitation of Solomon's dedication of the Temple, a unique occurrence. It presupposes some annual festival of kingship in Jerusalem. From this it appears that Jeroboam instituted a "Royal Bethel Festival" to substitute for the Royal Zion Festival and ensure the loyalty of the northern tribes. In all probability, Hosea refers to some such feast in Hosea 7:5 where he speaks of the "day of our king."

In Judah, an indication of the continued existence of this festival is afforded by the account of Josiah's great celebration of the Feast of Tabernacles, 2 Kings 23:1-3. There we read that the king went up at the head of a great procession and officiated at the ceremony of renewal of the covenant. Is it not possible to see the royal festival indicated in the procession and the cere-

monial renewal of the covenant, the two significant features of
the Feast of Tabernacles?

The second type of evidence for the Royal Zion Festival is
that contained in the Psalms. Of these, Psalm 132 and Psalm 89
give the clearest evidence, and in addition Psalm 78:65-72,
Psalm 24:7-10, Psalm 2, and Psalm 72 help to corroborate this
view.

From the nature of the historical evidence we have just discussed, it is clear that there can never be absolute certainty
about this festival. The best that can be hoped for is to show that
there is a high degree of probability in its favor and that it
faithfully interprets the biblical data. The evidence from the
Psalms is subject to the same qualifications.

At the outset several observations can be made about Psalm
132. First, it contains the two themes found in 2 Samuel 6 and 7,
the divine choice of Jerusalem as the site for the Ark (vss. 13-
14), and the choice of the Davidic dynasty (vs. 11). Second,
there are various hints of dramatization, the clearest of which are
the search for the Ark in verse 6, the procession in verse 7, and
the prayer for God to participate as the Ark is carried up, verse
8. Third, it is implied that this hymn was used repeatedly in
some ceremonial connected with kingship by the reference to the
contemporary Davidic king in verse 10. On the other hand, the
Psalm does not give any detailed account of how the celebration
took place, it does not demand any elaborate dramatization, and
it does not indicate that the festival was celebrated every year.

Now then, let us let the Psalm speak for itself and then see
if the setting it had in ancient Israelite worship can be reconstructed.

> 1. Remember, O Yahweh, for David
>   All his exertions,
> 2. That which he swore to Yahweh,
>   Vowed to the Mighty One of Jacob.

These two opening verses set the mood of the Psalm and
introduce its first theme. The worshipers are seeking to claim for
"David," the present Davidic king, the divine blessing earned by

the ancestor and founder of the royal house through the ful-
filment of his oath and vow.

> 3. I will not enter the tent of my house;
>   I will not ascend the couch of my bed.
> 4. I will not give sleep to my eyes,
>   Or slumber to my eyelids
> 5. Until I find a place for Yahweh,
>   A dwelling for the Mighty One of Jacob.

The historical books do not record any such vow on the part
of David, but simply the fact that he set out to bring the Ark to
Jerusalem. We evidently have here an independent tradition
from the life of David that for some reason was not included
in the history. His vow was certainly a strong one—to remain
outside his house and not to sleep at all until he brought the
Ark to a permanent shrine. One wonders how David kept his
vow during the three months the Ark was in the house of Obed-
edom the Gittite between the first and second attempts to move
it! (2 Samuel 6:11.) It might be easier to picture this vow as
the result of the failure of the first attempt and expressive of
David's determination to succeed the second time. The parallelism of the lines is particularly beautiful in this passage.

> 6. Lo, we heard of it in Ephratha;
>   We found it in the fields of Yaar.
> 7. Let us go into his dwelling,
>   Let us worship at his footstool.
> 8. Ascend, Yahweh, to thy resting place!
>   Thou and the Ark of thy strength!
> 9. Thy priests are clothed with righteousness,
>   And thy faithful ones shout aloud.

In this section are found the clearest clues to the interpretation
of the Psalm as a dramatic ritual. Verse 6 tells in brief the history
of the search for the Ark, and the recital of this verse may have
been accompanied by appropriate actions. The word Ephratha
can be interpreted in two ways. It may be a poetic form of
Ephraim and refer to the time when the Ark was located in the

shrine in Shiloh. "We heard of it in Ephratha" would mean, we remember its having been at Shiloh, but it has been lost to view for a long time now. Or it may mean Bethlehem. (Compare Micah 5:2, "But thou, Bethlehem Ephratah.") In that case, hearing of it in Ephratha would mean the searchers were on the right track and had heard of its actual location when they inquired in Bethlehem.

They finally found the Ark in Kiriath-jearim, "City of the Woods," poetically paraphrased here as the "fields of Yaar," that is, "fields of the wood." The search is ended and the joyful worshipers now proceed to form a procession to accompany the Ark to Jerusalem. They exhort one another to go to God's "dwelling," the tent prepared for the Ark, so they may worship at his footstool—at the Ark. But the Ark is not just a box to be carried off; it is a symbol and guarantee of Yahweh's presence, and since the procession cannot start until Yahweh wills it, they call on him to arise and go to Jerusalem, verse 8. The priests in charge of the Ark are clothed with sacred garments that express God's righteous dealings with his people, and the faithful members of the covenant community join the procession shouting for joy, blending their voices with the sound of the ram's horns. Just as David demonstrated the divine approval of Jerusalem when he took the Ark there, so the reigning scion of David's house is reminding the people of that fact by the re-enactment of the first procession.

> 10. For the sake of David thy servant
>   Do not turn away the face of thy anointed.
> 11. Yahweh has sworn to David;
>   He will not swerve from his truthfulness.
>   Of the fruit of thy body
>   I will place on thy throne.
> 12. If thy sons keep my covenant,
>   And my testimonies which I shall teach them,
>   Surely their sons for ever
>   Shall sit on thy throne.

Here the divine choice of David and the promise of kingship to his posterity are made the basis of a prayer for the reigning king, verse 10. Verses 11 and 12 recount the promise, bringing it forcefully before the assembled worshipers. In 2 Samuel 7 there is no mention of an oath. God's promise is stated simply in the first person, just as here in the last part of verse 11 and in verse 12. Evidently the solemnity of the oracle and the faithfulness of God gave it the force of an oath in the minds of the people. In Psalm 89:35, a cultic hymn of kingship, God's oath to David in this connection is also spoken of.

The shortness of the lines in 11b and 12b has led some scholars to suppose that one or more words have dropped out. The two verses, 11 and 12, are clearly parallel to each other and the alternation of long and short lines gives them a distinct poetic character that is evident even in translation. There is no justification for trying to emend the text here.

Verse 12 restates the terms of the promise: obedience and faithfulness on the part of the Davidic kings. This was a part of the original oracle, 2 Samuel 7:14-15, and was considered an essential element in the royal ideology. Second Samuel 7:14, however, does not mention a covenant and testimonies, but only says "if he commit iniquity." We have already seen that in the coronation of Joash the testimonies played a part (2 Kings 11:12), and that these testimonies are related to the idea of the covenant. This verse gives further indication that the two belong together.

> 13. For Yahweh has chosen Zion,
> He delights to dwell there.
> 14. This is my resting place for ever;
> There I am enthroned for I delight in her.
> 15. Her food I will surely bless;
> Her poor I will satisfy with bread.
> 16. And her priests I will clothe with salvation,
> And her faithful ones will shout and rejoice greatly.

Here is the other head of doctrine, the other dogma on which the Davidic throne rested, the choice of Jerusalem. God declares he will dwell there forever and will bless her both materially and spiritually. The faithful ones (the English versions read "saints") are those loyal to the covenant and to David. In verse 9 they were seen taking part in the procession and shouting aloud. In verse 16 the same verb, denoting shouting in the course of worship, is used in an intensive construction, rather feebly translated as "shout and rejoice greatly." The clothing of the priests also refers back to verse 9 and the procession.

> 17. There I will make a horn to sprout for David;
> I have lighted a lamp for my anointed one.
> 18. His foes I will clothe with shame,
> But on him will his crown shine.

The two themes are united in the conclusion. It is there in Jerusalem that the house of David will rule. His rule is expressed in two symbols, the horn, which indicates strength (compare Deuteronomy 33:17 and Luke 1:69) and the lamp, which was a sign that a house was still occupied, the scene of life. When Ahijah promised ten tribes to Jeroboam, he reserved one for the house of David so that God's servant might continue to have a lamp before God in Jerusalem, the city of God's choice (1 Kings 11:36). Finally, there is the splendor of the crown on the head of the Davidic king which is in contrast to the shame that covers his enemies.

Can the ancient festival be reconstructed on this basis? Certainly not in any detail, but an attempt is in order. The roads leading to Jerusalem have been crowded with pilgrims going up to the great fall festival. Excitement is in the air and a sense of awe as the hour for the re-enactment of David's procession draws near. The sacred Ark is in its place outside the city walls, and the king with a group of priests and royal companions go about searching until suddenly they find it. A shout goes up! "We heard of it in Ephratha, we found it in the fields of Yaar!" In response to the call to go up, a procession forms and the priests solemnly call on Yahweh to be present and to accompany the Ark as it goes up into the city. The king leads the procession, dancing and singing, and slowly they all wind their way amid joyful shouts through the gate and to the court of the Temple. There the two great passages, 2 Samuel 6 and 7, are read to the people, and in prayer God is called upon to fulfill what he promised to David and to Jerusalem, the city of David.

IV

Kingship and the Religion
of Israel

Since the ideology of the monarchy was so clearly theological in nature, it is likely that it had some effect on the whole of Israelite religious life. We can investigate only a few of the areas where it had influence, and those are the areas most closely related to the monarchy. What was the relation of the Sinaitic covenant to the Davidic covenant? What about the monarchy and the pagan religions? Many of the Davidic kings from Solomon on introduced pagan worship into Israel. How did this affect the main stream of Israelite thought? What happened to the idea of Yahweh as king? Was it crowded out, or did it survive? How does this royal ideology tie in with the idea of a coming Messiah? The last of these questions is of special importance for the Christian and will be dealt with in the next chapter. The others will be investigated in this chapter.

Recent scholarship has placed great emphasis on the importance of the covenant for Israelite religion. The comparison of the covenant with the suzerainty treaty of the ancient Near East as preserved in the Hittite texts has already been referred to in Chapter I in connection with the idea of the kingship of Yahweh. The biblical evidence that the conclusion of such a covenant is to be dated in the time of Moses is substantiated by the nature of "Israel" in its early history, for although Israel lacked racial unity since it incorporated certain "Canaanite" elements after the conquest (e.g., the Gibeonites, Joshua 9), it nevertheless had a unity. This unity was not so much political as it was religious, and it found its expression in loyalty to the amphictyony of tribes that worshiped the same God and had its center in a common shrine.[1]

In Deuteronomy 5 we find a ceremony that might be called a renewal of the covenant. Moses told the people that Yahweh made the covenant not with their fathers who were present at Sinai but with all of those who were present before him that day. That is to say that the covenant is a living reality which must be made real to each generation. In Joshua 24 a similar ceremony is recorded in which Joshua gathered all the people together at Shechem and made a covenant with them. The content of this chapter identifies the covenant made at Shechem with the Sinaitic covenant in all its essentials.

The covenant continued to be a living reality in Israel, and there were certainly more ceremonies of this type observed from time to time. Artur Weiser has investigated the terminology of the covenant festival and shown that it is reflected throughout the Psalms.[2] His conclusion is that the festival that celebrated and renewed the covenant is the point of origin of the vast majority of the Psalms and that these Psalms were the liturgy of that festival. Among the relevant psalm passages are the following:

> Blow the trumpet at the new moon,
> At the full moon, on our feastday.
> For it is a statute for Israel,
> An ordinance for the God of Jacob.
> He appointed it in Joseph for a testimony,
> When he went out over the land of Egypt.
>   (Psalm 81:3-5, A.S.V.)

> For he established a testimony in Jacob,
> And appointed a law in Israel,
> Which he commanded our fathers,
> That they should make them known to their children;

. . . . . .

[1] Noth, *The History of Israel*, pp. 85-97.
[2] Artur Weiser, *Die Psalmen* in *Das Alte Testament Deutsch*, pp. 18-29. Göttingen: Vandenhoeck and Ruprecht, 1950.

> That they might set their hope in God,
> And not forget the works of God,
> But keep his commandments.
>
> (Psalm 78:5, 7, A.S.V.)

The festival was at least in part a cultic drama in which the central element was the meeting of God with his people and the renewal of the Sinaitic covenant. In this sacrament of worship, the making real of God's word and his dealings with his people was dependent on God's self-revelation. Since the Ark was the visible throne of the invisible God, it probably played a central role in the coming of God's presence among his people. A minimum of dramatization would have sufficed for this, and there is no need to suppose there was an elaborate enactment of the events of Sinai.

Among the features of the festival, as found in the Psalms, were the theophany, God's appearance as on Sinai (Psalms 18:7-15; 50:3ff.; 68:1ff., etc.), the proclamation of God's name, particularly the name Lord of Hosts (Psalms 46:7; 48:8; 50:7; 81:10, etc.), the depicting of God's nature by the recital of his deeds of salvation (Psalms 66:5ff.; 81:7ff.; 89:5ff., etc.), and the declaration of his will and his judgment (Psalms 9:16; 11:4-7; 75:2-8; 98:9). Passages could be multiplied in illustration of these themes, but these brief references serve to indicate that the Psalms abound with the concepts that are to be found in connection with the covenant.

As we have seen in investigating the origins of the monarchy, the tribal league bound together by the covenant found itself faced with a very serious threat from the Philistines and sought to preserve itself by choosing a king. Saul operated largely within the framework of the old amphictyony, and David sought to strengthen his position by making Jerusalem the center of the covenant traditions. But the question arises, How did the covenant God made with David stand with respect to the Sinaitic covenant? Attempts have been made to show that the Northern State held to the Sinaitic while the South gave preference to the Davidic covenant, but the matter was certainly not that simple. The covenant with David has more resemblance to that made with Abraham than to the Sinaitic covenant. God called Abraham and gave him an unconditional promise of blessing. In a like manner, God bound himself to maintain the Davidic line on the throne, but from the first there was a moral obligation imposed on the king. If he sinned, he would be punished, but God would remain loyal to the covenant and not destroy the monarchy (2 Samuel 7:14-16). Over against these was the Sinaitic covenant binding the whole nation in obedience to God.

Before the Davidic monarchy was very old, however, it became the channel through which various pagan elements were introduced into the life and worship of Israel. Most conspicuous in the biblical account is the matter of Solomon's many wives (1 Kings 11:1-13).

Also in the reign of Solomon there was another area in which there was borrowing from Israel's neighbors. David had been prevented from building a permanent shrine for the Ark of the Covenant, and the work was entrusted to Solomon. Ernest Wright has shown in detail how the architecture of the Temple was borrowed wholesale from the Phoenicians.[3] For example, the shape of the Temple, the two free-standing columns in front of it, and the cedar lining of the interior are all typical of the temples of Israel's Phoenician and North Syrian neighbors. Interestingly enough, the Bible does not indicate that this provoked a reaction among those loyal to the traditions of Sinai. The Temple, for all its Canaanite architecture, was assimilated to the orthodox worship of Yahweh.

As time went on, the fertility cult of Canaan became an increasing force in the life of Israel. In the Northern Kingdom Jezebel actively supported the worship of Baal and persecuted the prophets of Yahweh (1 Kings 16:31-33; 18:4, etc.), and Queen Athaliah (2 Kings 8:18; 11:1) followed a similar course in the Kingdom of Judah. Periodic reforms were carried out in both kingdoms, but the worship of Baal always managed to reassert itself. One reason for this was the confusion of names of the deity, for Baal was a name also given to Yahweh in its meaning of "Lord." Hosea announced an end of this practice,

[3] G. Ernest Wright, *Biblical Archaeology*, pp. 140-141. Philadelphia: The Westminster Press, 1957.

saying that God would take the names of the Baalim out of the mouth of Israel (Hosea 2:16-17), and Yahweh would not be called Baal any longer. It has been mentioned earlier that Saul named one of his sons Ishbaal or Eshbaal (1 Chronicles 8:33).

The second chapter of Hosea is a good example of how the fertility cult was combated. Central to the chapter is the concept of Yahweh as husband of the nation, not the husband of the land as Baal was. In contrast to the wanton lovers and to the harlotry of the fertility cult stands the faithful husband whose actions cannot be controlled through the cult but whose blessing for his people is constant. Stress is laid on the fact that the gifts of nature come not from the Baalim but from Yahweh—the creator-God.[4] The prophetic attack on the syncretism practiced by the people consisted in using terms that the people could understand after first purging the terms of mythology and filling them with new content.

Since the discovery of the Ugaritic literature, there have been many efforts to demonstrate the similarities between Canaanite religious poetry and the Psalms.[5] Cultural and literary borrowings such as poetic form and similarities of vocabulary, while very important for a clear understanding of the literature of the Psalter, are not involved in the question of syncretism. On the other hand, the use of such Canaanite motifs as the sea serpent Leviathan in Psalm 74:14 and the coming of the storm God in Psalm 29 raise the question whether some definite acceptance of Canaanite beliefs may not have been involved. Where these themes occur, however, they appear not as alien elements but as harmonious features of Psalms that are thoroughly Yahwistic in nature. That is to say, they have been purged of their mythological significance and made to serve the purposes of the main stream of Israelite theology.

One illustration will demonstrate what is meant by this. In his reconstruction of the Festival of the Enthronement of Yahweh, Mowinckel developed in some detail what he considered to be

[4] Cf. H. W. Wolff, *Dodekapropheten, Hosea,* pp. 53f. Neukirchen, Kreis, Moers: Buchhandlung des Erziehungsvereins, 1958.
[5] John Hastings Patton, *Canaanite Parallels in the Book of Psalms.* Baltimore: The Johns Hopkins Press, 1944. Many other works might be cited.

the cultic myths of the festival. The first of these is that of the myth of creation and the fight with the dragon.[6] In the Babylonian myth of the creation, the god Marduk defeated the sea serpent Tiamat, who was the primordial salt ocean, and divided her body in two, forming the heavens of one half and the earth of the other.[7] Mowinckel cited Psalm 93, Psalm 95, and Psalm 96 among the so-called enthronement Psalms, and also Psalm 24, Psalm 33, Psalm 29, and Psalm 65 and Isaiah 42:10-17 as illustrative of this myth. Now the concepts of creation and of Yahweh's lordship over the sea by right of creation are certainly present here as elsewhere in the Old Testament, but they are not at all similar to the Babylonian myth. The difference is clearly illustrated in Psalm 95:5, "The sea is his, and he made it." In Babylon the "sea" existed before Marduk's fight with the monster; indeed the monster *was* the primeval salt sea, and the "creation" took place after the battle. Nor is there any hint in Psalm 95 of a fight between Yahweh and "chaos." This fight may be alluded to, however, in Psalm 89, one of the Royal Psalms, where the defeat of "Rahab" is mentioned. The echoes of a mythical combat are but faint; the myth has been demythologized by the religion of Israel. From the Psalms one can clearly draw only the teaching of Yahweh's creation of the world and his consequent power over it.

How much of this pagan influence must be blamed on the royal ideology will always remain problematical. From the time of Solomon, kings of the Davidic line were instrumental in introducing pagan practices into the life of the nation, but this was an abuse of the Davidic covenant, a perversion of the royal ideology. When these kings emphasized God's promise of everlasting duration of the line of David to the neglect of the moral demands of the covenant, they went counter to the Sinaitic traditions and countenanced paganism and a syncretistic development. When they were recalled to the ancient faith of Israel, they sought to purge the cult of these foreign elements. Syncretism in the sense of merging of divergent systems of thought, for

[6] Mowinckel, *Psalmenstudien II*, pp. 45-50.
[7] James B. Pritchard, ed., *Ancient Near Eastern Texts Relating to the Old Testament*, pp. 60-72. Princeton: Princeton University Press, 1950.

example, the fertility cult and the Sinaitic theology, did not take place in Israel. In the sense of the uncritical acceptance by many of beliefs inconsistent with normative Yahwism and in the sense of the adoption of nonessential forms and themes, it definitely did take place. In this development the ideology of the Davidic covenant could be used to protect the purity of the faith, or it could be abused so as to provide a channel for the entry of pagan elements.

One of the most difficult questions of kingship in the Old Testament is that of the date and significance of the Psalms dealing with the kingship of Yahweh. A characteristic phrase is "The LORD reigns," found in Psalms 93:1; 96:10; 97:1; and 99:1. Although this phrase is not found in Psalms 47, 95, and 98, they are generally included in any discussion of this problem since they also speak of Yahweh as king. Mowinckel contended that the correct translation of the Hebrew was "Yahweh has become king."[8] This translation and the whole hypothesis of Mowinckel were accepted by Leslie in his commentary on the Psalms.[9] Indeed he accepted it so wholeheartedly that he translated Psalm 47:7 that way with no explanatory note, although the Hebrew text reads "God" (Elohim) and not Yahweh, and there is a significant difference of word order![10] It is not sufficient to assume, as he does, that because "Yahweh" seldom occurs in this part of the Psalter a commentator is justified in restoring a supposedly original reading of "Yahweh" in place of the later "God" reading. Both this commentary and that of Oesterley[11] give a clear defense and exposition of Mowinckel's work.

It is extremely doubtful, however, that this translation can be maintained. The Psalms celebrate the *fact* of Yahweh's kingship, not its *beginning*, and the theory of the enthronement festival of Yahweh has met with increasing opposition in recent years. This is still, however, a much debated question and unfortunately too complex to be dealt with thoroughly within the limits of this work.

[8] Mowinckel, *op. cit.*, pp. 3-43.
[9] Elmer A. Leslie, *The Psalms*, p. 66. New York: Abingdon-Cokesbury Press, 1949.
[10] *Ibid.*, p. 66.
[11] W.O.E. Oesterley, *The Psalms*, p. 259. London: S.P.C.K., 1953.

In any case, the concept of Yahweh as king is to be found in the Old Testament during the period of the monarchy.[12] The Psalms of the kingship of Yahweh cannot be dated with any exactness, but fortunately Isaiah 6 gives us a firm date in the eighth century B.C. when we can be sure that Yahweh was thought of as king. It is not unlikely that these Psalms date from the period when the Royal Zion Festival was being celebrated in Judah. They may even be among the songs that belonged to that festival. In that case they served to remind the people that above and behind the earthly king was the heavenly King, creator of the world, the one who had set David on the throne and promised to uphold his posterity and maintain the Davidic monarchy. In the last analysis, the theory of a festival celebrating the enthronement of Yahweh is most effectively refuted by the proposed Royal Zion Festival, which fits the biblical data much better than the other festival and crowds it out of a place in the agenda of the Feast of Tabernacles by taking the first day, the day on which it was supposed to have been held.

It would appear from the foregoing that the ideology connected with the Davidic covenant had a rather unfortunate effect on Israelite religion. It obscured to some extent the Sinai theology and opened the door to an influx of pagan ideas and practices. To say this, however, is to state only one side of the case. The royal ideology was never meant to stand alone and at its best was a supplement to the Sinaitic covenant. The kings could be defenders of the faith as well as its perverters, witness Asa, Joash, Hezekiah, and Josiah. Moreover, while it is undeniable that the kings introduced idolatry and other pagan practices, it is hardly conceivable that in the absence of the monarchy these things would never have happened. Israel lived in too close proximity to her neighbors for all of her people to remain faithful to the religion of Moses and Sinai.

Then, too, there is a more positive side of the royal ideology that needs to be examined, the elements which led to the expectation of a perfect king of David's line, a Messiah.

[12] See Kraus, *Psalmen*, Vol. I, pp. xliii, 197-205.

V

The Messiah

Perhaps here more than in any other field on which this study has touched there is need for careful and precise definition of terms in order to avoid confusion. By the term "Messianic" I mean the expectation of an ideal king of the Davidic line, who will fulfill all the hopes that attached to the line as a result of God's promises to David. This definition limits the field to the biblical material and the later Jewish literature and excludes any use of the term to describe the elaborate royal ideologies of the other lands of the ancient Near East. Only in Israel, moreover, was there any expectation of a future ideal king.

The most important work on the Messiah to appear in English in recent years is the monumental volume of Sigmund Mowinckel, *He That Cometh*.[1] In that book Mowinckel takes the position that a true Messianic hope did not arise in Israel before the Exile. He insists the Messiah is an eschatological figure, an element in the expectation of a restored Israelite state. Clearly there could not be a hope for a restoration before there was need for one—that is before the destruction of the Judean state and the end of the Davidic monarchy.[2] No one can deny that that was the case after the Exile, but what about the age of the monarchy? To say that the hope of the Jewish people after the fall of the monarchy was conditioned by the circumstances under which they lived is also to say that the hope of the people during the time when kings reigned was condi-

---

[1] Sigmund Mowinckel, *He That Cometh*. Nashville: Abingdon Press, 1956.
[2] *Ibid.*, p. 155.

tioned by their circumstances. It is not to say that in the earlier period no one looked beyond the limits of that era to a happier time in the future. The hope they had was in accord with the times in which they lived, but it can still have been a Messianic hope.

An investigation of the Israelite royal ideology and the Messianic passages led Mowinckel to the conclusion that the king in the former and the Messiah in the latter are identical in all their main features.[3] At the same time he concluded that practically all the Messianic passages are to be dated in the postexilic age. (Any attempt to establish the date of the passages he discusses would both be too technical for this discussion and expand it far beyond its limits.) But even if it be granted that all the passages he dates after the Exile are correctly dated, there is sufficient material for us in the two oracles he admits to be pre-exilic, that is, Isaiah 7:10-17 and 9:1ff. Mowinckel argues that since these passages are pre-exilic they are probably concerned with historical kingship rather than with the Messiah, for there was no expectation of a Messiah before the Exile.[4] This is to assume as evident what he was setting out to prove. No Messianic ideology existed before the Exile, so since these passages are pre-exilic, they cannot deal with the Messiah in spite of the fact that they are sayings about the ideal future king of the line of David.

To this we must say, No! If Isaiah 7:10-17 and 9:1ff. deal with the ideal king of David's line and are pre-exilic, then in the period before the Exile there was some expectation of an ideal future king, a Messiah. Of course, some features of this hope were modified by the terrible experiences of the end of the state and the Exile, but the postexilic hope was in its essentials the same as the pre-exilic hope and was the natural development of the latter. In order to demonstrate this let us examine the Davidic royal ideology as given in 2 Samuel 7, in one of the Royal Psalms, Psalm 2, in the oracle of Isaiah in chapter 9:1ff., and in a

[3] *Ibid.*, p. 20.
[4] *Ibid.*

Messianic oracle considered by Mowinckel to be postexilic, Jeremiah 23:5f. (paralleled in 33:15f.).

The Nathan oracle has been discussed in Chapter II, and here a brief summary of its major elements will serve the purpose of comparing it with the other passages. In the oracle God promised David a successor on the throne, one who would be the physical descendent of David and thus continue the dynasty. This future king will be the adopted son of God. The dynasty will continue to rule and the throne will be secure forever. The king, however, is liable to error, and if he sins God will punish him, but not by destroying the dynasty. Finally, the accomplishment of this promise is dependent on the initiative of God himself.

The Second Psalm is concerned with establishing the king's right to rule in the face of strong opposition, verses 1-3, and is consequently best under·   od as part of a ceremonial of either a coronation of a new k·   ng or a periodic celebration of kingship such as probably too k place in the Royal Zion Festival. The king is a descendar·   of David and sits on the throne in Jerusalem, verse 6, wr ere he has been installed by God to rule over the people. He is, in addition, the adopted son of God.

> 7. The Lord said unto me, Thou art my son,
>   This day have I begotten thee.

This is undoubtedly the formula of adoption. Since a grown man, or at least a boy old enough to hold the royal power, is being addressed the begetting could not mean a physical generation, for quite obviously the king was not physically begotten on the day of his coronation.

Eternal duration of the kingdom is not explicit in this Psalm, but the king is to have the nations for his inheritance and the ends of the earth for his possession, verse 8. Also, the terms in which the rulers are admonished in verses 10-12 indicate that his rule is not going to be merely transitory. Nor is there any indication that the king is liable to sin. The principles that underlie his kingship are those that are characteristic of God's kingship, the righteousness and justice so often spoken of in the other Royal Psalms. Throughout the Psalm the power behind the throne—that is, the almighty power of Yahweh—is evident, and there is not any question but that he is the one who will see that these promises are carried out. Once again the elements of the royal ideology are evident, this time in a hymn of the ceremonial of kingship in the period after the reign of David.

In Isaiah 9:1-7 the prophet gives an incomparable picture of the future hope of the nation. The Assyrian king Tiglath-Pileser III had incorporated certain areas of the old Israelite state into his empire, and now the territory of Zebulun and Naphtali, the mountains of Transjordania, and the plain leading down to the sea were lost to God's people. Yet even in such a time of mourning the hopes that centered around the house of David were a source of joy and expectation to the people. Out of the darkness comes light, and out of defeat victory and joy. The reason for this is the Davidic king who is born and who will usher in the golden age. Not that a highly developed eschatology in the sense of later Jewish doctrine is to be found here. Yet the "end" is implied. After this king reigns what then? The question is clearly out of place for there shall be no end of the increase of his government and of peace. He shall rule in righteousness "from henceforth even for ever," verse 7. Clearly a turning point in history is pictured; the shame and suffering of defeat are past, and the glorious future breaks into history.

The end of verse 6 gives the amazing titles of this king:

> And his name shall be called
> Wonderful Counselor, Mighty God,
> Everlasting Father, Prince of Peace.
> (R.S.V.)

There are two tendencies in the interpretation of these terms that must be avoided. On the one hand it is easy to explain them away by putting them in terms of the style of the courts of the ancient world, hyperboles that expressed the concepts of divine kingship. On the other hand they can be divorced from their historical setting altogether and used as indications of the deity of the Messiah. Somewhere between these two extremes lies the right path. Wilhelm Vischer has indicated this path in his study of the relation of these Isaianic oracles to the Royal Zion Festival.[4] The Davidic king is the adopted son of God, and ruling in God's name he bears the titles that express the nature of God as revealed in the Davidic covenant.[5] The terminology used in this oracle can be illustrated by reference to passages in the Royal Psalms.

Wonderful Counselor. The king's counsel includes his decisions and judgments in fulfilling his office, and if he is to make the right decisions that will result in victory in war and in the prosperity and peace of his people, divine help is needed. In 2 Samuel 7:9, God reminded David that he was with him in all that he undertook, and in one of the Royal Psalms (20:4) a petition is made for the king that God will fulfill all the king's counsel. The wonderful, awe-inspiring nature of the works of God is mentioned in two of the Royal Psalms.

> 72:18 Blessed be the Lord God, the God of Israel
> who alone doeth wondrous things.
> 89:5 And the heavens shall praise thy wonders,
> O Lord.

Mighty God. This might also be translated "god-like hero." Through the Davidic dynasty God had indeed shown deeds of might, and they are mentioned in the Royal Psalms.

> 20:6 Now I know that the Lord saveth his anointed;
> He will answer him from his holy heaven
> With the saving strength (heroic deeds of
> salvation) of his right hand.
> 21:13 Be thou exalted, O Lord, in thy strength,
> So will we sing and praise thy power
> (heroic might).

The application of this term and the next one to the Messiah indicates that he is more than human, but a detailed explanation is very difficult.

[4] Wilhelm Vischer, *Die Immanual-Botschaft im Rahmen des königlichen Zionfestes,* Theologische Studien, 45. Zurich: Evangelischer Verlag AG., 1955.
[5] *Ibid.*

Everlasting Father. Both parts of this term are of great importance for the Davidic covenant. The king is God's adopted son, and God is his father (2 Samuel 7:14). In addition, references to the everlasting nature of the throne are frequent. Once again, the Royal Psalms can be drawn upon for illustrative material.

> 89:26 He shall cry unto me, Thou art my father.
>   29 His seed also will I make to endure for ever.
> 21:4 He asked life of thee, thou gavest it him,
>   Even length of days for ever and ever.
>   6 For thou makest him most blessed for ever.

Prince of Peace. The kingdom of Yahweh will restore perfect order and harmony through the rule of his adopted son. Peace and righteousness are mentioned together in Psalm 72:7. In addition, if Isaiah 9:7, where justice and righteousness are mentioned, is to be taken as an explanation of the nature of this rule, there is much in the Royal Psalms to support the parallel, for they are full of these two concepts, for example, Psalms 89:14; 72:3, 7; 101:1.

In Isaiah 9:7 the throne and kingdom will be established. This is a familiar thought in the material relating to David's house.

Second Samuel 7:16. And thy house and thy kingdom shall be made sure for ever before thee; thy throne shall be established for ever.

Psalm 89:14. Righteousness and justice are the foundation of thy throne.

Finally, at the end of verse 7, we are reminded that God stands behind these promises and will see that they are fulfilled. "The zeal of the Lord of Hosts will perform this."

In this oracle, all six of the elements found in the Nathan oracle are present: the promised king, the king as descended from David (on the throne of David, verse 7), the king as son of God (verse 6), everlasting duration of the throne, the demand for justice, and God's activity as the decisive element in it all. As for justice, we have moved far beyond the Nathan oracle, where the likelihood of the king's sinning was considered. Here the king will uphold justice and righteousness, and there is no question of his breaking faith with Yahweh. This is a clear indication of the fact that this passage has moved beyond the actual historical situation toward the ideal future age. In this oracle we see the Messiah in the full sense of the term.

The oracle of Jeremiah recorded in two slightly different forms in 23:5-6 and 33:15-17 presupposes the destruction of the monarchy and the exile of the people. After the reign of Josiah (639-609 B.C.), the Davidic kings in Jerusalem were far from fulfilling the demands of the covenant, but the hopes that attached to that line continued and now took the form of a hope for the restitution of kingship.

> Behold the days come, saith Yahweh
> That I will raise unto David a righteous Branch,
> And he shall reign as king and deal wisely,
> And shall execute justice and righteousness in the land.
> In his days Judah shall be saved,
> And Israel shall dwell safely;
> And this is the name by which he shall be called,
> "Yahweh is our Righteousness." Jeremiah 23:5-6.

"Behold the days come" (23:5) and "In those days and at that time" (33:15), while possibly not eschatological in the restricted sense of later Jewish doctrine, clearly look beyond the immediate future and envisage a time of blessing that will be permanent (33:17). Can the familiar elements of the Nathan oracle be found here also? The whole point of the passage is the coming rule of a scion of David's house, a successor to David, and his descendent (vs. 5). As in Isaiah 9, the king will rule in righteousness and justice, and there is no indication that he may sin or break the covenant. In 33:17 an additional verse is found that promises eternal duration to the kingdom, this idea being put in the terms that there shall never be cut off from David a man to sit on the throne. This carries the implication that the "righteous Branch" will not be the only Messianic king, but rather the first of a long line. Conspicuously absent is the concept of God's being the father of the king and the king God's adopted son. On the other hand, that is inherent in the Davidic covenant from the first and therefore here by implication. All this future restoration is explicitly dependent on God's initiative, "Behold, I will raise unto David a righteous Branch" (23:5; cf. 33:15).

Of particular interest is the idea of a Branch, or shoot, which is also to be found in Isaiah 11:1 and in Zechariah 3:8; 6:12. Out of the stump of the tree that has been cut down, out of the devastated line of David, will yet come life, a shoot that will bring blessing to the people. Here is a picture of a new beginning and yet of continuity with the past.[6]

The study of these various passages seems to bear out the view advanced at the outset. The royal ideology of the Davidic dynasty as set forth in the Nathan oracle is essentially that which is reflected in the Second Psalm, one of the hymns of the Israelite festival of kingship. In the realm of history, however, the ideals of the monarchy were never realized, for time and again the reigning kings fell short of the demands of the covenant and disappointed the hopes of the people. Yet that hope persisted in spite of these unrealized elements of the royal ideology, as Mowinckel termed them.[7] This gave the theology of Israelite kingship a forward drive that is certainly akin to a fully developed eschatology, although admittedly its development was gradual. With the work of Isaiah, whose prophecies are steeped with the royal ideology, the concept of a coming Messiah clearly appears, a Messiah who differs from the expected king of the house of David as he was awaited in earlier times only in that he is to a larger extent a figure of the future age.

After the passing of the monarchy from the stage of history, the age-old hope came to center in the longing for the restoration of kingship under a Messianic king essentially identical with the hoped for scion of David's line as seen in the pre-exilic materials. It is then no abuse of terminology to speak of those

---

[6] For a discussion of this term see Mowinckel, *op. cit.*, pp. 160ff., and the commentaries.

[7] *Ibid.*, pp. 451-452, additional note 1.

parts of Scripture that deal with the Davidic king as "Messianic" as long as they are seen in their proper historical context and not taken as literal descriptions of the person and work of Jesus the Messiah. They are indispensable for an understanding of who he is and what he has done, but they do not begin to contain all the meaning of the Messianic office as it is seen in him.

An Exposition of
the Royal Psalms

The ground covered in Part I provides a comprehensive picture of the background of the Royal Psalms and opens the way to their detailed study. It has been seen that the institution of kingship in Israel came into being late in the history of the ancient world and later than the other major institutions of the nation Israel. It was characterized at first as spiritual, for the first two kings held office by virtue of a special gift of the Spirit. After David, however, the charisma was transferred to the whole dynasty, an unbroken line of Davidic kings that ruled until the Exile in 587 B.C. It appears highly probable that the choice of the Davidic dynasty and of Jerusalem as the religious center of the nation was proclaimed and celebrated regularly at a great religious festival, and most indications point to the first day of the Feast of Tabernacles as the occasion of this Royal Zion Festival. The Royal Psalms fit this picture and are easily intelligible as parts of the ceremonial of the festival. In addition, these Psalms show many points of contact with the Sinaitic covenant, demonstrating that the covenant made with the whole nation

69

was not in conflict with that made with David. The Psalms also illustrate the forward drive of the royal ideology, the assurance that some day a perfect king of the house of David would sit on the throne in Jerusalem. Through the disappointments of history this assurance became an eschatological hope, but from the first it was Messianic.

In the following pages all the Royal Psalms are presented except Psalm 132, which received full treatment in Chapter III. In addition, the "Last Words of David" are included, for this very old poem (2 Samuel 23:1-7) contains the royal ideology in an early form. Each Psalm is translated directly from the Hebrew in an attempt to bring out the meaning clearly. It will be obvious that this translation cannot compete with the literary excellence of the standard English translations of the Psalms. Brief, but it is hoped, sufficient, justification is given for the few emendations of the text that are accepted. No attempt is made to cite all the commentaries that have been used, particularly those in German.

Psalm 2

THE CORONATION OF GOD'S ANOINTED

1. Why do the nations rage?
   And the peoples plot vain things?
2. Kings of the earth gather,
   And rulers meet together
   Against Yahweh and against his Anointed.
3. "Let us break their bonds,
   And cast from us their cords."

4. He who sits in the heavens laughs,
   The Lord mocks them.
5. Then he speaks to them in his wrath,
   And in his anger he terrifies them.
6. "But I myself have set my king
   On Zion my holy hill."

7. I will recount the ordinance of Yahweh.
   He said to me, "Thou art my son;
   This day I have begotten thee.
8. Ask of me and I will give
   Nations for thy inheritance,
   And for thy possession the ends of the earth.
9. Thou shalt break them with an iron scepter;
   Like a potter's vessel thou shalt shatter them."

10. And now, O kings be wise;
    Be instructed, O judges of the earth.
11. Serve Yahweh in fear,
    With trembling kiss his feet.[1]
12. Lest he be wroth and you perish in the way,
    For his anger is kindled easily.
    Blessed are all who trust in him!

[1] Cf. R.S.V.

The structure of this Psalm is plain and uncomplicated; it falls naturally into four strophes of approximately the same length. In the first of these, verses 1-3, the unrest and threatened rebellion of the subject nations are depicted. Over against this is the picture of God in stanza 2, where his purpose and his power are contrasted with the feebleness of the nations, verses 4-6. Next the Davidic king speaks and repeats the divine promise on which his power is based, verses 7-9, and finally, in verses 10-12 the rulers are exhorted to submit themselves to Yahweh and his anointed one before it is too late.

In attempting to reconstruct the way in which the Psalm was recited in ancient times, it is not necessary to assign the various strophes to different speakers, for they are all appropriate in the mouth of the king. As was shown in Chapter V in connection with the question of Messianic doctrine, this Psalm displays the features of the Davidic royal ideology, and so it could easily have been a part of the agenda of the Royal Zion Festival. There is no reason, however, why it could not also have served as a part of the coronation ritual as well as a part of the ritual of the annual festival of kingship. This twofold use is probably the most satisfactory interpretation of the Psalm.

Verses 1-3. The Psalm begins with a forceful rhetorical question that at once sets the mood of great activity and the universal scope of the psalmist's theme. The nations are in turmoil and are making grandiose plots, but all that they do is in vain. Then in the following two verses this theme is developed and explained. The rulers of the nations are eager to free themselves from subjection to the Davidic king in Jerusalem and the God who has given that king his power, but because the revolt is directed against the God who controls all of creation, it is doomed from the start; it is in vain. Older commentators tried to find some historical situation that would fit this dramatic scene, and in view of the contrast between the wide scope of the Psalm and the very limited extent of the Judean kingdom, they explained the Psalm as an imitation of models to be found in the courts of the great empires. There is no need to go far in order to find a model, however. The empire of David reached far beyond the bounds of Israelite territory and long after it fell apart the Davidic kings in Jerusalem must have continued to remember its greatness and hope for its restoration. Moreover, if the cultic nature of the Psalm is recognized and attention given to its repeated use in worship, either annually or at the coronation of a new king, there is no need to look for a particular historical situation to which it belongs. This view would place the Psalm in the Judean kingdom some time after the age of David, but most probably early rather than late.

Verses 4-6. With a bold anthropomorphism, the poet depicts the reaction of Yahweh to the plots of the subject nations; he laughs and mocks the petty rulers who will not acknowledge his sovereignty. At the same time, the poet shows God's nature by the use of the two terms, "the one seated (i.e., enthroned) in heaven" and "the Lord." The true king of all the world is God, the sovereign Lord, who has his throne in heaven and rules through his deputy in Zion. When the Lord addresses these rebels he speaks in anger and strikes terror into them. The words he speaks are not themselves terrible, but they produce this reaction in the rebels because they express clearly the divine choice of the king of David's line and the approval of Zion in pronouncing it God's own holy hill. The revolt is not against a human ruler but against God. The occurrence of these two elements, choice of David and choice of Jerusalem, places this Psalm squarely in the traditions of Davidic kingship and within the framework of the Royal Zion Festival.

Verses 7-9. Leslie adopted Gunkel's very drastic emendation of the text of 7a, "I will take thee up into my bosom."[2] This highly arbitrary alteration of the text is totally unnecessary as it makes good sense as it stands. The word "ordinance" prompted this emendation because of the difficulty of interpreting it, but if we follow the explanation that it is the same as the "protocol" or "testimony," that is, the documentary record of the divine choice of the Davidic dynasty, the meaning of the line becomes quite clear.[3] The king now speaks in the first person, recounting

[2] Leslie, *The Psalms,* p. 92.
[3] See above p. 42.

the divine oracle on which his kingship is based. Yahweh has made the king his son by adoption, using the formula, "Today I have begotten you." Addressed to a grown man, or at least a young man, this could not have meant physical procreation but an act of the divine will in elevating the king to a unique relation to God. This is completely in agreement with the oracle in 2 Samuel 7:14, which was so important for the Davidic kingship.

Then comes God's promise to honor the king's request for world dominion. The nations will be his inheritance and the uttermost parts of the earth his dominion. Here is one of the unrealized elements in the royal ideology that gave it a forward look and aided in the development of the Messianic doctrine. This hope for the extension of God's kingdom to all the nations was not realized through the ancient monarchy and was transferred to the days of the coming king. The harsh features of this rule, breaking the nations with an iron scepter and shattering them like a potter's vessel, expresses in ancient oriental imagery the universal judicial power of the king. Similar figures of speech were used in Egypt and Mesopotamia. By a simple change of the vowels the text of verse 9 can be read as "shepherd them" rather than "break them." The biblical text used by the writer of the New Testament Apocalypse read it this way as is seen from Revelation 2:27; 12:5; and 19:15. Since, however, the reading of the Masoretic text gives a better parallel to the next half line, it has been followed in the translation given above.

Verses 10-12. The concluding stanza is a stern warning to the earthly rulers to submit themselves to Yahweh, and, by implication, to his deputy, the king in Jerusalem. The proposed change in verse 11 carries out the imagery of submission to a world ruler and is a good parallel to the first half of the verse. The Hebrew text of this line has provoked great discussion and many suggested translations. The k.j.v., followed in this by the a.s.v., reads "kiss the son." The word translated "son" is *bar*, which, while it means "son" in Aramaic, cannot mean this in Hebrew. The Hebrew word for "son" has just been used in verse 7 of this Psalm and would certainly have been used here if that had been the meaning intended. The texts of the ancient translations show that they too were confused by the word. If the first two words of verse 12 in the Hebrew are moved to the beginning of the second line in verse 11 the resulting text reads "Kiss his feet with trembling." The present state of the Hebrew text can be explained as the result of a simple disarrangement of the text in very ancient times. Since the Hebrew does not make sense as it now stands, any translation means a correction of the text, and this one is as good as any and better than most. The picture of divine wrath and imminent disaster is balanced by the final line, which breaks the confines of the metrical structure of the Psalm with the joyful shout, "Blessed are all who trust in him!"

This Psalm gives one of the greatest pictures to be found anywhere in Scripture of the sovereignty of God and God's activity in history as he works out his purpose. This alone commends it as rich material for study, but the position of the Psalm in the development of Messianic doctrine and the New Testament use of the Psalm give it added value for the Christian. The early church interpreted the plotting of Herod and Pilate in terms of the revolt of the first stanza (Acts 4:25ff.). And Paul in his address in Antioch of Pisidia (Acts 13:33) as well as the writer of the letter to the Hebrews (1:5) saw in the sonship of Jesus Christ the fulfillment of the sonship of the Davidic king as promised by God. In him the unrealized elements of the royal ideology became reality.

Psalm 18

THE KING'S SALVATION

(A Hymn of Praise)

1. I exalt[1] thee, O Yahweh, my strength.
2. Yahweh is my rock, my retreat, my deliverer,
   My God, my Rock in whom I trust.
   My Shield and the Horn of my salvation, my Refuge.

(A Cry for Help)

3. I call on Yahweh, who is worthy of praise,
   And from my foes I am saved.
4. The billows[2] of death overwhelm me;
   The streams of oblivion terrify me.
5. The cords of the underworld surround me;
   Before me are the snares of death.
6. In my distress I call to Yahweh,
   And to my God I cry out.
   From his palace he hears my voice,
   And my cry comes unto his ears.[3]

(God Appears)

7. And the earth shook and quaked,
   And the foundations of the mountains trembled.
   They shook, for he was wroth.
8. Smoke went up from his nostrils;
   Fire from his mouth consumes.
   Coals burned before him.

[1] Compare Psalms 30:2; 145:1; Isaiah 25:1.
[2] Read with 2 Samuel 22:5 "billows" instead of "cords."
[3] Omit "before him" with 2 Samuel 22:7 as overburdening the line.

9. And he spread apart the heavens and came down;
   Thick darkness was under his feet.
10. And he rode on a cherub and flew;
    He swooped on the wings of the wind.
11. He made darkness his hiding place,
    His covering[4] round about,
    The darkness of waters, thick[5] clouds.
12. From the brightness before him clouds pass,
    Hail and coals of fire.
13. And from[6] heaven Yahweh thundered;
    The Most High uttered his voice.[7]
14. He sent his arrows and scattered them,
    He shot out[8] lightning and confused them.
15. And the bottom of the sea[9] was seen,
    And the foundations of the land revealed.
    At thy rebuke, O Yahweh,
    At the blast of the breath of thy nostrils.

(God Delivers)

16. He sends from on high and takes me,
    He draws me from the deep waters.
17. He delivers me from strong foes,
    And from those who hate me, for they are stronger
        than I.
18. They were before me in the day of my misfortune,
    But Yahweh was my support.
19. And he brought me forth to a wide place;
    He delivers me, for he delights in me.

(The Righteousness of the King)

20. Yahweh rewards me according to my righteousness,
    Requites me according to the cleanness of my hands.

[4] Read "covering" instead of "pavilion."
[5] Read "thick(ness)" for "clouds."
[6] The preposition probably has the archaic meaning "from" in this case, rather than "in."
[7] 2 Samuel 22:14 omits "hail and coals of fire." It was probably copied from the verse above.
[8] This reading is based on Psalm 144:6.
[9] This is the reading in 2 Samuel 22:16.

21. For I have kept the ways of Yahweh,
    And have not rebelled against my God.
22. For all his ordinances are before me,
    And his statutes I do not put away from me.
23. Also I have been straightforward with him,
    And I have kept myself from iniquity.
24. And Yahweh rewarded me according to my righteous-
    ness,
    According to the cleanness of my hands before his
    eyes.[10]

(*God's Faithful Dealings*)

25. With the loyal thou art loyal,
    With the perfect man thou actest perfectly.
26. With the pure thou actest purely;
    But with the perverse thou art unyielding.
27. For thou savest the oppressed people,
    And humblest the haughty eyes.
28. For thou lightest my lamp, O Yahweh,
    My God, thou makest my darkness bright.
29. For by thee I run through a troop,
    And by my God I leap a wall.
30. He is the God, whose way is perfect,
    The message of Yahweh is tested.
    He is a shield for all who trust in him.

PART II, VERSES 31-46
THE ROYAL WELFARE

31. For who is a God besides Yahweh?
    And who is a Rock but our God?

(*God Prepares the King for Battle*)

32. As for God, he girds me with strength,
    He makes my way blameless.

---

[10] This verse may be a doublet to verse 20.

33. Who makes my feet like hinds' feet,
    And makes me stand on the heights.[11]

34. Who teaches my hands to war,
    Makes my arms to draw a bow of brass.

35. And thou gavest me the shield of thy salvation,
    And thy right hand sustains me,
    And thy favor makes me great.

36. Thou enlargest my steps under me,
    And my ankles do not shake.

(The King is Invincible in War)

37. I pursue my foes and catch them,[12]
    And do not look back until I finish them.

38. I crush them and they cannot rise,
    They fall under my feet.

39. And thou girdest me with strength for war;
    Thou makest my adversaries bow under me.

40. And my foes have turned the shoulder to me,
    And those who hate me I destroy.

41. They cry, but there was no savior,
    To Yahweh, but he does not answer them.

42. And I pulverize them like dust before the wind,
    Like the filth of the street I crush them.[13]

43. Thou savest me from the strife of the peoples;
    Thou makest me head of the nations.
    A people that I have not known shall serve me.

44. When they hear with the ear they shall heed me.
    Sons of the foreigner shall feign obedience to me.

45. Sons of the foreigner are exhausted,
    And come out of their hiding places.

46. Yahweh lives! And my Rock is blessed!
    Exalted be the God of my salvation!

[11] The Hebrew reads "my heights."
[12] 2 Samuel 22:38 reads "destroy them."
[13] Thus 2 Samuel 22:43.

CONCLUSION, VERSES 47-50

47. As for God, he grants me vengeance,
    Even subdues[14] peoples under me.
48. My deliverer from angry foes.[15]
    Thou settest me on high from those who rise against
    me.
    Thou deliverest me from the man of violence.
49. Therefore I will laud thee among the nations, O
    Yahweh,
    And I will sing to thy name.
50. He multiplies the salvation of his king,
    And keeps covenant with his anointed,
    With David and his seed for ever.

The textual criticism of this Psalm is complicated by the fact
that it is also recorded in 2 Samuel 22 in a version that differs
from the Psalm in very many details. In addition many phrases
from this Psalm also occur in Psalm 144. An attempt to determine
the original text would exceed the scope of this volume, and the
above translation is intended only as a clarification of the text of
Psalm 18 as it is now found in the Hebrew Bible.[16]

The Psalm falls into two distinct parts, verses 1-30 and 31-46
with a conclusion, verses 47-50. The differences between the
two parts are sufficiently great to lead some commentators to regard them as separate Psalms. Leslie correctly regards the Psalm
as a unit but assigns it to the time of Josiah.[17] The work of
Cross and Freedman has made clear that the Psalm is much

[14] Compare Psalm 144:2.
[15] This is the reading of the Greek.
[16] An excellent attempt to establish the original text of this Psalm is found
in the article by Frank Cross and David Noel Freedman, "A Royal Song
of Thanksgiving," *Journal of Biblical Literature*, LXXII, pp. 15-34. Philadelphia: The Society of Biblical Literature and Exegesis, 1953. Many of
their suggestions are incorporated in the foregoing translation, but others
which were based more on stylistic grounds appear too subjective to be included here.
[17] Leslie, *op. cit.*, pp. 259 f.

older than that, for otherwise it is impossible to explain its textual peculiarities.[18]

The prominence of the theophany in verses 7-15 and the significant position of the king, especially verses 32-45, show that this Psalm is anchored in the worship of Israel, probably in the autumn festival. The revelation of God in the theophany places the Psalm in the Israelite covenant tradition, and the royal aspects connect it with the celebration of the divine choice of the Davidic dynasty. That is to say, the Sinaitic covenant and the Davidic covenant are united in this Psalm. The overall impression is that of divine help and blessing over a longer period of time rather than one specific deliverance and this is in keeping with the view that the Psalm was one of the festival hymns of Israel. The alternation of tenses in the translation is an approximation of the use of the tenses in the Hebrew.[19]

PART I, DELIVERANCE FROM DISTRESS

After a brief introduction in the form of a hymn of praise to Yahweh (verses 1-2), the poet depicts his distress and cries out to Yahweh for salvation (3-6). The king faces no concrete threat in these verses, but his peril is expressed in terms of the underworld, Sheol, which appears in verse 4 under the figure of raging waters and in the next verse in the figure of a hunter with cords and snares seeking his prey. Then follows the central theme of part one, the theophany, which is given in language that reminds the reader of such other passages where God appears as Exodus 19, 2 Kings 19, Isaiah 6:1f., and Judges 5:4f. The theophany is best explained not as a foreign element introduced by the poet as a piece of colorful antiquarian literature but as a living theme in the traditions of the covenant community and the means by which the people were made to realize the reality of what God had done in the past. Probably a very little dramatization would have been enough to bring the Sinai tradition to life for the worshiper. In the theophany God's power

---

[18] Cross and Freedman, *op. cit.*, p. 20.
[19] The extent to which the tenses give a clear indication of the time of the action is debatable. Cf. Cross and Freedman, *op. cit.*, pp. 19-20.

is depicted, but Yahweh himself remains hidden from view, concealed by the darkness and the thick clouds that indicate his presence. Among the many allusions to the theophany at Sinai, verse 15 is reminiscent of the Exodus and the crossing of the Red Sea, "The bottom of the sea was seen."

In the following verses, 16-19, God delivers the one who has cried to him. While still in general terms, this is not so vague as the situation in verses 3-6. Here "strong foes" and "those who hate me" put the danger in terms of earthly enemies rather than Sheol. Verse 16 with the use of the verb "draw" (mashah) in all probability alludes to Moses, who was also drawn from the waters, and this too brings the king's deliverance into the framework of the history of salvation. Verses 20-24 set forth the righteousness of the king. Leslie interpreted this as "Deuteronomic," that is to say, good fortune shows God's approval and misfortune his punishment.[20] But this concept and the terminology used here were not monopolies of the writers of Deuteronomy and the Deuteronomic histories. Instead of being a profession of self-righteousness, this section is a confession of the experience of God's covenant loyalty toward those who keep his commandments. After the position of the king had been threatened (verses 3-5), his righteousness, as a part of the royal welfare, must be affirmed and confirmed in the worship. With an easy transition, the Psalm passes on to the climactic confession of God's faithfulness in his dealings with individuals, verses 25-26, with the people, verse 27, and with the king, verses 28-29, and culminates in the note of praise of God whose ways are perfect, whose word is without dross, the shield of those who trust him.

PART II, THE ROYAL WELFARE

The mood of this part of the Psalm is quite different from that of the first part, but the theme of God's salvation is the same. In contrast to the urgency of the cry of distress in verses 4-6, there is noticeable here the detachment that is the result of the successful outcome of an undertaking. The implication of verses 33 and 36 is that the Psalm was written at a time when wars

[20] Leslie, *op. cit.*, p. 261.

were still fought on foot, the chariot not yet having been adopted in Israel. This agrees with the situation in the time of David. When David defeated Hadadezer king of Zobah he captured 1700 horsemen, but kept only enough horses for 100 chariots, a start on a mechanized army, and hamstrung all the rest (2 Samuel 8:3-4). Apparently even David felt uncertain about the use of chariots in the Israelite army. Later, of course, they were widely used (1 Kings 22:29ff., for example). The king looks back at the preparation God gave him for battle, verses 32-36, and the invincible force with which he defeated his foes, verses 37-42. Since these enemies of the king are ones who called to Yahweh, they are probably to be identified with domestic adversaries such as those who gave David so much trouble until he could consolidate his power. They submit themselves readily, coming out of their hiding places to acknowledge the sovereignty of God's chosen king. The Psalm closes with praise of the God who has wrought victory and will again give victory and welfare to his Anointed One. That indeed is the message and the purpose of the cultic use of this Psalm. In verse 49 there is a vow of the king to praise Yahweh among the nations, and in verse 50 the Psalm ends with explicit reference to the royal welfare, the salvation of the Davidic line. God increases the king's salvation and shows covenant loyalty and love to David his anointed king in the maintenance of his house from generation to generation.

In this Psalm the role of the king as bringer of God's blessings to the chosen people is quite prominent. He does not effect an integration of nature and society, like that practiced in the fertility cults, but rather by his loyal observance of the requirements of the covenant relationship he is able to receive the God-given victory and prosperity that form the basis of the welfare of his people. If the view that this Psalm fits into the cultic celebration of the covenant relationship by uniting the Davidic and Sinaitic covenants is correct, then it serves to underline the importance of the king in the cult, his central role in the worship of pre-exilic times in Jerusalem. This Psalm found its fulfillment and its antithesis in Jesus who, when he was surrounded by his enemies, told his disciples he could call for more than twelve legions of angels to fight for him but whose way of victory was by submission to God's will that the Scriptures might be fulfilled (Matthew 26:53-54). God did not leave his soul in Hades (Acts 2:27) (cf. vss. 5, 16). Because he was obedient even unto death, he was exalted in power as Lord of all creation (Philippians 2:8-11). God delivered him because he delighted in him. He became head of the nations, foreigners bowed in obedience and at the last every knee will bow to him and every tongue confess him Lord.

Psalm 20

A PRAYER FOR THE KING

1. May Yahweh answer thee in the day of distress:
   May the name of Jacob's God protect thee.
2. May he send thee help from the sanctuary,
   And support thee from Zion.
3. May he remember all thy offerings,
   And accept thy whole burnt offerings.
4. May he give thee according to thy heart,
   And fulfill all thy councils.
5. We shall rejoice in thy salvation,
   And raise a banner in the name of our God.
   May Yahweh fulfill all thy requests!
6. Now I know that Yahweh saves his anointed!
   He answers him from his holy heavens
   By the saving might of his right hand.
7. Some (trust) in chariots and some in horses,
   But we hold in remembrance the name of Yahweh our
   God.
8. They kneel and fall down,
   But we stand and arise erect.
9. Save the king, O Yahweh!
   Answer[1] us in the day when we call!

The older view was that this Psalm was a prayer on behalf of
the king before he went out to war. Leslie accepted this view.[2]
But if this were so, the situation would have been more
clearly indicated. This Psalm almost certainly belongs to the
festival of kingship as one of its hymns.

According to verse 3 a sacrifice has probably just been made
on behalf of the king, and the prayer of the congregation for

[1] Thus the Greek. The Hebrew reads "may he answer us."
[2] Leslie, The Psalms, p. 264.

the king that begins with verse 1 either follows the sacrifice or accompanies it.

The first four verses were perhaps recited by one person, for verse 5 seems to indicate that the whole congregation takes up the prayer. The "name" of God is given an important place in the Psalm, verses 1, 5, and 7. It represented the making known of God's nature and his activity in history. This is clear in the explanation of the meaning of his name in Exodus 3:13-15, where God tells Moses to tell the children of Israel that Yahweh is the name of the One who sent him and that he is the God of Abraham, Isaac, and Jacob.

Furthermore, God promised in Exodus 20:24 that in every place where he caused his name to be remembered he would come to the people and give his blessing. It was only natural that after Solomon built the Temple on Zion this promise would be attached in a particular way to the Temple as the place where God said, "My name shall be there" (1 Kings 8:29). Solomon's dedicatory prayer is full of references to the fact that while God's name dwells in the Temple, he himself is so great that "heaven and the heaven of heavens" cannot contain him. In this way God could be thought of as present on Zion in a special way without being limited to a house made with hands.

Many Israelites were undoubtedly tempted to pervert the divine promise to be present where his name was called upon and follow the heathen practice of using the name of God as magic in order to try to force him to do their bidding. But this was clearly prohibited in the third commandment, Exodus 20:7. Instead, the Old Testament concept of calling on the name of Yahweh meant invoking his presence (Psalm 20:5, 7), and honoring him in worship (Psalms 7:17; 9:10; 18:49; 68:4). God is sovereign, and while he honors his promise he is not bound by the mere recitation of forms and empty phrases.

Zion plays a central role as the place where God's name dwells and the site from which God's help originates. This is another indication that this is one of the Royal Psalms. As in the other Royal Psalms, the Jerusalem sanctuary and the Davidic king are intimately related.

In verse 3 the verb translated "accept" is literally "make fat" or "accept as fat" and this is no doubt a technical term of the cult. In verse 5 the setting up of a banner can best be explained as another part of the ritual. The royal salvation expected here consists of answering the king, protecting him, sending help, supporting him, giving him the desires of his heart, and fulfilling his plans.

There is a definite break in the Psalm between verses 5 and 6, and since there are no rubrics, the reader can only guess at what took place in the interval. There was probably some indication of a favorable answer to the petitions of the first part of the Psalm through a sign connected with the sacrifice or through an oracle given to a prophet serving in the Temple. The mood of the last part of the Psalm is in any case one of certainty that Yahweh has heard the prayer and will faithfully answer it from heaven by his great saving power. Other nations rely on chariots and horses, but the Israelites, though they fight on foot, are saved because of their faithfulness to the revelation of God's being known to them through the divine name.

The last line is difficult. If the Hebrew punctuation is observed, it must be translated, "Save O Yahweh, May the King answer us in the day when we call," but this divides the line unevenly and destroys the meter. If the line is divided evenly and the word "king" read with the first half, it is best to take it as referring to the earthly king rather than to Yahweh as king, and that translation has been adopted above.[3]

While it is difficult to place this Psalm in a definite cultic festival, it fits the general view of kingship that has been shown to characterize Psalms 2 and 18 and would be appropriate in the royal festival that seems to have taken place at the autumn feast.

The religious content of the Psalm is on a very high level. The dependence of the people and their king on Yahweh and their assurance that loyalty to God is of greater importance than trust in armaments show a lofty conception of the need to subjugate political and military affairs to the will of God. References

[3] Both Leslie and Oesterley read it that way. Leslie, *op. cit.*, p. 264; Oesterley, *The Psalms*, p. 172.

to the history of God's dealings with his people are not as prominent in this Psalm as in others, but they are present nonetheless in the mentioning of the God of Jacob, of Zion, God's chosen sanctuary, and of Yahweh's Anointed, who follows in the line of the Davidic kings.

Psalm 21

BLESSINGS FOR THE KING

(God Has Answered the King)

1. O Yahweh, in thy strength the king rejoices,
   And in thy saving acts how greatly he is glad!
2. Thou hast given him the desire of his heart;
   What his lips asked thou hast not withheld.
3. For thou dost meet him with blessings and good
   fortune;
   Thou settest on his head a crown of gold.
4. Life he asked of thee; thou gavest it to him;
   Length of days for ever and ever.
5. Great is his glory in thy salvation;
   Thou hast placed honor and might upon him.
6. For thou makest him a source of blessing for ever.
   Thou hast made him glad with the joy of thy presence.
7. For the king is trusting in Yahweh,
   And in the steadfast love of the Most High he shall
   not be moved.

(God's Victory in War)

8. Thy hand finds out all thy foes;
   Thy right hand finds out those that hate thee.
9. Thou makest them like a furnace of fire
   When thou appearest, O Yahweh.
   In thy wrath thou devourest them like fire.[1]
10. Thou destroyest their fruit from off the earth,
    And their seed from among the children of men.
11. For they planned evil against thee;
    They plotted mischief which they could not fulfill.

[1] The emendation of this line follows generally that suggested in Kittel, *Biblia Hebraica*, Fourth Edition.

12. For thou makest them turn the shoulder;
    With thy bow string thou aimest at their faces.

(*A Petition*)

13. Arise, O Yahweh, in thy strength!
    We will sing and praise thy might!

This Psalm has often been regarded as a royal liturgy of thanks
for victory in war.[2] It contains, however, no concrete references
to the victorious outcome of a war, and it is not primarily a Psalm
of thanks; the theme is the royal welfare, which is the result
of God's blessing and can be maintained only by the continuation of that blessing. The mood of the Psalm is appropriate to
a celebration that looks back on Yahweh's gracious bounty bestowed on the king and seeks its renewal, and it is therefore best
understood as a part of the festival of the king.

The first six verses are a prayer offered by the priest or prophet
who was leading the worship, and in this prayer the blessings of
God to and through the king are called to mind. It reaches its
climax in verse 7 when the confidence of the king in God's un-
changing faithfulness is affirmed. In this verse both God and the
king are spoken of in the third person; this indicates a change
in speaker from the preceding verses, probably the congregation
taking up the prayer in response.

God's strength and his salvation, or saving acts, are the theme
of the prayer (vs. 1). They have been given to the king in answer
to the petitions in which his lips expressed his heart's desire, the
fulfillment of his hopes and aspirations for his reign. He has been
crowned and his rule has begun auspiciously. David the founder
of the royal house had prayed

> Now therefore let it please thee to bless the house of thy
> servant, that it may continue for ever before thee; for thou,
> O Lord Jehovah, hast spoken it: and with thy blessing let
> the house of thy servant be blessed for ever.
>
> (2 Samuel 7:29, A.S.V.)

---

[2] Oesterley, *The Psalms*, p. 173.

In the same way the present king of David's line had asked for long life (vs. 4) so that he might be able to carry out his plans for the nation. God's promise is "ask of me and I will give thee" (Psalm 2:8), so the confidence is expressed here that the prayer for long life has already been heard and answered. The honor and might God has given him are obvious in his regal bearing, and he is the source of the prosperity and blessing that the people are now enjoying. All this is possible because the king has absolute trust in God's loyalty to his covenant.

Judah's history was characterized by the necessity of the little nation's fighting for its life against enemies on every side, so it is natural that God's help in war would be an indispensible part of the divine blessing. Since the king is God's chosen instrument, and he fights in Yahweh's name, the victory is not his but Yahweh's. Consequently, the battle is pictured in terms that remind the reader of God's appearances to his people, the theophanies, several of which are recorded in the Psalter. In verse 9, God conquers in fire which devours his enemies (compare Psalm 97:3-5), and in verse 12 he shoots his arrows as he does in Psalm 18:14. The repeated emphasis on finding the enemies in verse 8 points to elusive bands of raiders who would pillage and then retreat before the defensive forces could engage them in battle. However, God fights for his people, and will destroy the fruit and the seed of their enemies. Such events as these occurred over and over again throughout the course of Judah's monarchy, but in view of the use of this Psalm in worship, the events given here are not to be understood as those of any one time but as an expression of assurance of victory through God's power, an assurance that was founded on the covenant with David.

The king's hope was fixed on God and as a consequence he was able to rise above the ebb and flow of current events. God's promises to David and to his house might not be fully realized in any one age of Israel's history, but faith in God's covenant carried the nation forward in the expectation of one who by God's grace would fulfill their longings for blessing and prosperity. The king is happy under God's protection and in the life of strength and salvation that God gave him.

Psalm 45

A ROYAL WEDDING

1. My heart overflows with a good theme.
   I will recite my poem to the king.
   My tongue is the pen of a skillful writer.

(To the Bridegroom)

2. Thou art most beautiful among the sons of man;
   Grace is poured on thy lips,
   Therefore God has blessed thee for ever.
3. Gird thy sword on thy thigh, O warrior,
   Thy honor and thy majesty!
4. ([1]) Prosper, ride on in the cause of truth,
   Meekness and righteousness.
   Thy right hand shall teach thee fearful things
5. Thy arrows are sharp—peoples fall under thee—
   In the heart of the king's enemies.
6. Thy throne, like God's, is for ever and ever;
   A righteous scepter is the scepter of thy kingdom.
7. Thou lovest righteousness and hatest evil.
   Therefore God, thy God, has anointed thee
   With oil of gladness in preference to thy companions.
8. Myrrh, alloes, cassia are all thy garments;
   From ivory palaces harps make thee glad.
9. Daughters of kings are among thy lovers;
   Thy consort stands at thy right hand in gold of Ophir.

(The Bride)

10. Hear, O daughter, see and give ear,
    And forget thy people and the house of thy father.

---

[1] The words "and in thy majesty" were evidently copied by mistake from the line above. They should be deleted. There are many textual difficulties in the Hebrew text of this Psalm but the meaning is clear in general.

11. And let the king desire thy beauty,
    For he is thy lord—bow down before him.
12. Daughter of Tyre, the rich of the people seek thy
    favor with gifts.
13. All glorious the king's daughter enters,
    Clad in cloth of gold.
14. In bright clothing she is led to the king.
    The virgins, her companions, follow and are
    brought to her.
15. Accompanied by gladness and rejoicing
    They enter the palace of the king.
16. Instead of thy fathers shall be thy sons;
    Thou shalt make them princes in all the land.
17. I will make thy name to be remembered in all genera-
    tions;
    The people will praise thee for ever and ever.

The interpretation of this Psalm is the subject of continuing disagreement. The view that it is an allegory of Christ and the church has been widely rejected, and recent commentators follow one of two general directions. They either term it a secular wedding hymn written for a royal pair no longer identifiable with certainty,[2] or at the other extreme, with those who regard the whole Psalter as more or less a book of verses underneath the golden bough, call it a cultic lyric for the "sacred marriage" in Jerusalem.[3] Neither of these extremes is correct. On the one hand, there is no evidence at all that hierogamy, a ritual marriage of the god, was practiced in Israel. Any practice so completely contrary to Israelite religion would certainly have been denounced by the prophets if it had ever occurred.[4] On the other hand, the Psalm is colored by a high moral earnestness and a sense of religious responsibility too evident to permit the designation "secular." It portrays, moreover, a marriage, an event which

[2] Oesterley, *The Psalms*, p. 250. Hans Schmidt, *Die Psalmen*, in *Handbuch zum Alten Testament*, Vol. 15, p. 85. Tübingen: J.C.B. Mohr, 1934.
[3] Although not representing this view, Mowinckel has a good discussion of sacred marriage in *He That Cometh*, pp. 23-24, 42-43, 48, 50, 53-55, 456.
[4] Bright, *A History of Israel*, p. 205.

even in secularized twentieth-century society has at least religious overtones, and most certainly cannot have been secular
in ancient Israel. Not only so, but it is the wedding of a king,
probably a Davidic scion, which is being celebrated, and nothing
that touched his life and the matter of the continuation of the
dynasty so intimately could have been secular. Quite probably
this hymn was used regularly for royal weddings and became
a standard item in the cultic poems of kingship.

The singer begins with a masterful introduction that sets the
literary tone of the poem. He is bubbling over with the theme
of the royal wedding, and with the sure strokes of a skillful
court scribe he presents his work to the king without hesitation.
The first part of the Psalm, verses 2-9, portrays the king in his
splendor. God's blessing has resulted in the monarch's being
beautiful in form and graceful in speech. He is a skillful warrior
who subdues his enemies and maintains the cause of truth, meekness, and righteousness. Here in verse 4 are set the limits of the
king's warfare. Truth, righteousness, and meekness impose moral
standards that guard against wanton aggression and bloodshed.
Since the king was probably rather young at the time of marriage,
the picture of him as a warrior gives more the future ideal than
the past achievement.

Verse 6 has caused much difficulty. The writer of the Epistle
to the Hebrews cited this verse in 1:8 as evidence of the deity
of the "Son" as part of his superiority to angels. In recent years,
however, the verse has been used to prove that the reigning
monarch in Israel was deified and that the "pattern" of divine
kingship was accepted there. This is the only passage in the Old
Testament that supports such a view, and to build up an elaborate
ideology on one verse is a perilous task. To be sure, David is said
to be like the Angel of God (2 Samuel 14:17, 20) and even like
God (Zechariah 12:8), but he never is called God. As discussed
above, Isaiah 9:6 should be translated "Godlike Hero." The word
elohim, God, in this verse is usually read as being addressed to
the king. Oesterley found in this an indication that the king in
Israel was regarded as divine, just as in Egypt and Babylon,
but held that the divinity that attached to the king was the

result of the "will and act of Yahweh."[5] In this way, belief in Yahweh as the only God in Israel could be safeguarded. The view of Hans Schmidt is similar.[6] He stressed the way in which the picture of the king built to a climax with the result that he was addressed even as "God," a word the Israelite did not find easy to use when he spoke of his king. Leslie modified the force of the word by translating it as "divine one."[7] The translation given above takes *elohim* not as meaning the king, but as a metaphorical expression in which the human throne is compared to that of God and is promised eternal existence like that of the divine throne. However it is translated, it indicates a view of kingship that is striking when compared with the rest of the Old Testament.

Verses 6b and 7 again stress the moral character of the king and connect this morality with the designation of the monarch by anointing with holy oil, signifying the bestowal of spiritual gifts. Verses 8 and 9 depict the splendor of the king's palace and his harem and lead to a climax in the picture of the royal bride arrayed in gold of Ophir and standing at the king's right hand. The climax provides the transition to part two.

The latter part, verses 10-17, addresses the new queen with words of welcome and admonition. She is to forget her homeland and content herself with being a wife to the king of the land to which she has come and whose people bring her rich gifts. If, as has been suggested, the queen for whom this was written was Jezebel,[8] this is indeed ironic. Certainly there were daughters of Tyre who married kings of the line of David, and there is no compelling reason for making this a hymn of the Northern Kingdom. Verses 13-15 describe the splendor of her attire and the magnificence of her ladies in waiting as they accompany her. Verse 16 again returns to the theme of becoming a part of the national life; the sons she is expected to bear will be princes, and as queen mother she will have greater power through them than she ever had through her father in her home-

[5] Oesterley, *op. cit.*, p. 253.
[6] Schmidt, *op. cit.*, p. 253.
[7] Leslie, *op. cit.*, p. 266.
[8] Schmidt, *op. cit.*, p. 87.

land. Finally, the poet proclaims that her name will be immortal and that enduring praise will be hers. Unfortunately for her fame, her name does not appear in the poem. In a hymn designed to be used again and again in the ceremonies connected with the royal house, no one name would be appropriate. The queen's true fame consisted not in having her own name remembered but in contributing to the continuation of the house and the name of David.

Since this hymn was a part of the cultic literature of the Davidic monarchy, it is Messianic in the same sense that the other Royal Psalms are; that is, it reinforces the concept of God's blessing on David's house that was to culminate in an ideal king who would fulfill all the hopes of the people for righteousness and justice. It reaches forward toward the one who can truly be called God, as the Epistle to the Hebrews clearly saw.

Psalm 72

(Blessing and Righteousness)

    1. O God, give thy justice to the king,
       And thy righteousness to the king's son.
    2. He shall judge thy people in righteousness,
       Thy poor in justice.
    3. The mountains shall raise up welfare for the people,
       And the hills righteousness.[1]
    4. He shall vindicate the poor of the people;
       He shall save the sons of the oppressed,
       And crush the oppressor.
    5. May he live as long as the sun shines,[2]
       And the moon from age to age.
    6. He comes down like rain on the mown grass,
       Like the showers that water the earth.
    7. Righteousness[3] shall spring up in his days,
       And great peace till the moon is no more.

(The Extent of the Kingdom)

    8. He shall rule from sea to sea,
       And from the river to the ends of the earth.
    9. Before him the dwellers of the wilderness shall bow,
       And his foes shall lick the dust.
   10. Kings of Tarshish and the Isles
       Shall bring gifts.
       Kings of Sheba and Seba
       Shall present tribute.
   11. Yes, all kings shall bow to him;
       All the nations shall serve him.

[1] The Hebrew reads "in righteousness."
[2] Following the Greek. Hebrew has "they shall fear thee."
[3] The Hebrew reads "the righteous one."

(The Salvation of the Poor)

>12. For he delivers the poor when he cries,
>The oppressed whom there is none to help.
>13. He pities the poor and needy,
>And saves the life of the needy
>14. From oppression and violence he redeems their soul,
>And their blood is precious in his eyes.
>15. May he live and to him be given gold from Sheba,
>And prayer be made for him continually.
>Always will he be blessed.

(A Prayer for Blessing)

>16. May there be plenty of grain in the land,
>Abundance on the hill tops.
>May its fruit blossom like Lebanon,
>From the city like grass of the earth.
>17. May his name be for ever,
>His name flourish as long as the sun.
>They shall be blessed in him;
>All nations shall call him happy.

(Doxology)

>18. Blessed be Yahweh God, God of Israel,
>Who alone doth wonderful things.
>19. And blessed be his holy name for ever,
>And may his glory fill all the earth.
>Amen and Amen.

With its expression of justice as the basis of the king's rule and the picture of dominion over other nations, almost universal dominion, this Psalm has many similarities to the Royal Psalms already discussed, and like them it fits very well into the Royal Zion Festival.

The Psalm falls naturally into four sections. In the first, verses 1-7, the king's reign is characterized as one of righteousness and of blessing. In the next part, verses 8-11, the ideal dominion of

God's king is described in terms typical of the great empires of the ancient world, while in part three, verses 12-17, the salvation of the poor man and his consequent gratitude to the king form the introduction to the prayer of the common people for the royal blessing, verses 16-17. A doxology, verses 18-19, rounds out the thought and concludes the Psalm. Verse 20 is prose and is not an integral part of the Psalm.

Part one, 1-7. In the prayer that opens the Psalm, God's gift of righteousness is recognized as the basis of prosperity. The expression "king's son" does not necessarily indicate that the king is a young ruler only recently come to the throne but merely that he is a scion of the royal family. He must concern himself with the needy, the oppressed, in order to preserve the social equilibrium of his kingdom. He is to do this perpetually; indeed it is to be the practice of the dynasty to which he belongs in each generation, with the result that righteousness and peace will be as natural and as certain as the forces of nature—the seasonal rains, and the waxing and waning moon. It is probably better to read the verbs in this section as expressing wishes rather than statements, but the Hebrew may be read either way.

In the next section, verses 8-11, the phraseology of the courts of the great empires is evident. Like the rulers of Mesopotamia, the Judean king will rule from sea to sea, and from the Euphrates at the center to the farthest bounds of the earth. Although Tarshish in Spain, the isles of the Mediterranean, and the South Arabian lands of Sheba and Seba were never under the rule of Israel, this is not an expression of megalomania but an acknowledgment of God's universal rule and the corollary that God's chosen king will exercise that rule in righteousness and peace. This is one of the unrealized elements in the Davidic ideology that marks the early stages of Messianic hope.

The consequences of the world rule of the righteous king are found in the spread of righteousness throughout the realm (vss. 12-14), the prosperity of the poor (not the king) and his prayer for the king (vs. 15), and the fruitfulness of the land with abundance of grain, fruit, and grass (vs. 16). The nations acknowledge his rule with joy and call him blessed, wishing him enduring fame. In this way the divine promise to Abraham, Genesis 12, is fulfilled through the Davidic king.

The doxology in verses 18-19 rounds out the hymn on the thought with which it began—that it is God who works his purpose out through the king of David's line—and with a prayer for the coming of God's universal rule.

Psalm 89

LAMENT FOR THE HOUSE OF DAVID

1. Thy[1] steadfast love, O Yahweh, I shall sing for ever.
   From age to age I shall make known thy faithfulness
   with my mouth.
2. For thou[2] hast spoken, Let steadfast love be built up
   for ever.
   The heavens, thou settest thy truthfulness in them.
3. I have made a covenant with my chosen one,
   I have sworn to David my servant,
4. I shall establish thy seed for ever,
   And I shall build thy throne for all ages.

(A Hymn of Praise to the Creator)

5. And the heavens praise thy works, O Yahweh!
   Even thy faithfulness in the assembly of holy ones.
6. For who in the clouds is like to Yahweh?
   Who resembles Yahweh among the sons of the gods?
7. God is to be feared in the council of the holy ones,
   Great and dreadful above all around him.
8. Yahweh, God of Hosts, who is like thee?
   Thou[3] art mighty, And thy faithfulness surrounds thee.
9. Thou art ruler over the swelling of the sea;
   When his waves rise thou stillest them.
10. It is thou who didst smite Rahab like a carcass;
    With a strong arm thou hast scattered thy enemies.
11. Thine are the heavens, yes, thine the earth.
    The world and what fills it, thou hast founded.
12. North and South, thou createdest them;
    Tabor and Hermon rejoice at thy name.

[1] This reading follows the Greek.
[2] Following the Greek. Hebrew has "I have said."
[3] Hebrew has "YAH."

13. Thy arm is valorous,
    Thy hand is strong, thy right hand high.
14. Righteousness and justice are the base of thy throne;
    Steadfast love and truth are before thy face.
15. Blessed are the people who know the trumpet sound;
    O Yahweh, in the light of thy face they shall walk.
16. In thy name they joy all the day,
    And in thy righteousness they are lifted up.
17. For thou art the glory of their strength,
    And in thy favor is our horn exalted.
18. For our shield belongs to Yahweh,
    And to the Holy One of Israel our king.

(The Covenant with David)

19. Then didst thou speak in a dream,
    To thy faithful ones and saidst,
    I have set a crown[4] on a warrior,
    I have raised a choice man from the people.
20. I have found David my servant;
    With my holy oil I anointed him,
21. With whom my hand is firm.
    My arm also will strengthen him.

(a. God's Promises)

22. No enemy shall oppress him,
    Nor shall the sons of evil afflict him.
23. And I will crush his enemies before him,
    And those that hate him I will smite.
24. But my truthfulness and steadfast love are with him,
    And in my name is his horn exalted.
25. And I shall set his hand on the sea,
    And his right hand on the rivers.
26. He shall call to me, My father art thou,
    My God and the Rock of my salvation.
27. Truly I shall make him my firstborn,
    Most high over the kings of the earth.

[4] This is a conjecture. Hebrew has "help."

28. Forever will I keep (with him) my steadfast love,
    And my covenant is confirmed with him.
29. And I shall establish his seed for ever,
    And his throne like the days of the heavens.

(b. the Moral Condition of the Covenant)

30. If his sons should forsake my instruction,
    And not walk in my ordinances,
31. If they violate my statutes,
    And do not keep my commandments,
32. Then I shall punish their transgression with a rod,
    And their iniquity with stripes.
33. But my steadfast love I will not take[5] from him,
    Nor will I be false to my faithfulness.
34. I will not profane my covenant,
    And what went from my lips I will not change.

(c. Permanence of the Covenant)

35. One thing have I sworn in my holiness,
    And shall I lie to David?
36. His seed shall be for ever,
    And his throne like the sun before me.
37. Like the moon it shall be established eternally,
    A true witness in the heavens.

(Lament for David's House)

38. But thou hast rejected and despised;
    Thou art wroth with thy anointed one.
39. Thou hast annulled thy servant's covenant;
    Thou hast profaned his crown to the ground.
40. Thou hast breached all his walls;
    Thou hast made his fortified cities desolate.
41. All who pass by in the way plunder him;
    He has become a reproach to his neighbors.
42. Thou hast lifted up the right hand of his foes;
    Thou hast made all his enemies rejoice.

[5] This follows the reading of 2 Samuel 7:15.

43. Yes, thou hast turned his sword back,[6]
And hast not made him stand in battle.

44. Thou hast made an end to his honor,[7]
And hast hurled his throne to the ground.

45. Thou hast shortened the days of his youth,
Thou hast covered him with shame.

46. How long, O Yahweh? Wilt thou remain hidden for
ever?
Will thy wrath burn like fire?

47. Remember, O Lord, what my life span is,[8]
For what vanity thou hast created all the sons of men.

48. Who is the man who shall live and not see death?
Shall deliver his life from the grip of Sheol?

49. Where is thy former steadfast love, O Lord,
Which thou didst swear to David in thy truthfulness?

50. Remember, O Lord, the reproach of thy servant;
I have carried in my bosom all the contentions[9] of the
peoples,

51. With which thy foes taunt thee, O Yahweh,
With which they taunt the footsteps of thy anointed.

52. Blessed be Yahweh for ever! Amen and Amen!

The unity of this Psalm is striking in view of the diversity of
mood and literary form of its various parts. Although Oesterley
regarded it as composed of three originally independent parts
that were later combined into one Psalm, he pointed out that
these component parts have been joined together in a skillful
and appropriate manner to form a unified whole for use in
liturgical worship.[10] The parts, according to his analysis, are first,
a hymn of praise, verses 5-18, the celebration of the Davidic
covenant, verses 3-4 and 19-37, and a lament over the downfall
of the monarchy, verses 38-51.[11] This would mean that verses

---

[6] The meaning of the Hebrew is uncertain.
[7] The meaning of the Hebrew is uncertain.
[8] The Hebrew text is uncertain here.
[9] The Hebrew has "mighty."
[10] Oesterley, *The Psalms*, pp. 396, 402.
[11] *Ibid.*, p. 397.

3-4 were separated from their original context by the compiler and placed near the beginning of the Psalm in order to give it more unity. This may be. As the Psalm now stands, however, verses 3-4 form an excellent introduction to the whole, and any rearrangement of verse order would mar the literary perfection of the Psalm. Whether some or all of the parts of the Psalm led an independent existence before they were brought together is uncertain. The material is ancient and could have been taken directly from songs traditionally used in worship for the composition of the Psalm in its finished form.

As it now stands, the Psalm is the lament of the congregation over the decline of the Davidic monarchy. Section two is for the most part a poetic rendering of the prose oracle in 2 Samuel 7, the theological basis of David's kingdom. Just as 2 Samuel 7 was surely used to remind the people of God's promises to David, so this Psalm was most probably used in the Royal Zion Festival toward the end of the Judean kingdom when the festival was no longer a time of joy, but a time to lament the low estate of David's house and to plead with God to fulfill his promises.

The Psalm opens with a song of praise for Yahweh's covenant love, a concept so important in the Royal Psalms. It is paralleled by his faithfulness. In particular, this faithfulness is to be seen in God's covenant and his oath to David in terms of the familiar ideas of establishing his seed and building his throne to last throughout all generations.

The first major part opens with a reaffirmation of the supremacy of Yahweh over the other divine beings, "the sons of the gods," verse 6. The pantheon is spoken of also as "the assembly of holy ones" and the "council of holy ones" in verses 5 and 7. This is similar to the more dramatic picture of God among the gods found in Psalm 82, where he rebukes them for their impotence. These contemptuous references to the various gods do not mean that other gods were accepted alongside of Yahweh, but that in this way they were denied any power and reduced to objects of ridicule even in the eyes of those who had trusted in them. This method was also used by the great prophets (e.g., Isaiah 46;1-7; Jeremiah 2:9-13). Yahweh's supremacy to these gods that are no gods is seen particularly in his superior power and his faithfulness, verses 7-8.

The ancient theme of the defeat of the primeval monster is used in verses 9-10 as a further illustration of Yahweh's greatness. It is he who stilled the raging of the primeval sea when the earth was without form and void and darkness was upon the face of the deep, and it is he who split open the monster Rahab. This Rahab is perhaps to be identified with the monster Tiamat in the Babylonian story of "creation," for the two seem to have played the same role—the chaos which must be overcome before order can be established. In Isaiah 30:7 and Psalm 87:4 Rahab is used to designate Egypt, the great enemy from which Israel was delivered in the Exodus. Isaiah 51:9-10 makes the specific connection between God's smiting Rahab, the sea monster, and bringing his redeemed through the sea. Possibly this same idea of God's salvation is reflected in Psalm 89:10; certainly it was in the mind of those who sang this hymn after the return from the Exile.

In celebration of this victory, it is proclaimed that Yahweh is ruler over heaven and earth by virtue of the fact that he established them. Moreover, North and South are his, and the mountains of Tabor and Hermon rejoice when they hear his name. Since the discovery of the literature of the ancient city of Ugarit which preserves much of the mythology of the ancient Canaanites, attention has been drawn to the sacred mountain Saphon, a Levantine Olympus. This mountain, located in the north, gave its name to the direction north in the Hebrew language, and various attempts have been made to find mention of it in the Old Testament. A reference to it seems to occur in Psalm 48:2 where Mt. Zion is said to be "on the sides of the north" (A.S.V.). This can also be translated "in the far north" or "higher than Saphon." Mt. Zion is clearly not in the far north on any geographical view of the Middle East so some connection with this old Cannanite sacred mountain is probable. The Psalmist can bestow no higher praise on Zion than to give her supremacy over the holy mountain of the Canaanites. Now in Psalm 89 the situation is somewhat different. *Saphon* is coupled with the "south" as comprising two areas or directions, and it probably is best translated as "north," although the connotations of the ancient holy mountain are undoubtedly involved. Yahweh is supreme over all the gods, for he has created the mysterious north where the mountain of the gods was thought to be located. The kingship of God is explicitly mentioned in the reference to God's throne in verse 14, and perhaps also in verse 18, although the terse style makes translation difficult. In the latter part of the line, "our king" can be read in apposition to "the holy one of Israel," or it can be read as a parallel to "our shield" in the first half of the line. In the latter case the line would then read as follows:

> For our shield is Yahweh's,
> Our king belongs to the Holy One of Israel.

There are indeed many allusions to Canaanite religion in the first part of this Psalm but they indicate clearly how the Old Testament faith overcame the temptation to compromise with paganism, and preserved the belief in the supremacy of the Creator God. In comparison with his might and his goodness, the gods of the surrounding peoples are seen to be nothing at all.

Part two, verses 19-37, recounts the divine choice of David. Victory over his enemies, verses 22-23, God's support, verses 24-25, and the continuance of blessing to his posterity on the throne, verses 28-29, are all promises that are repeated here in this hymn of the Royal Festival. Verses 30-34 summarize the moral condition of the covenant, loyal obedience to the divine will, and lay stress on the fact that although God will punish wrong doing he will not profane his covenant or change his promise. The similarity of this passage to 2 Samuel 7:14-16 is so great that the text of verse 33 is usually corrected on the basis of 2 Samuel 7:15. Whatever the relation of the two passages to each other may be, both were rooted in the same worship tradition. The concluding verses of this part of the Psalm, 35-37, stress the enduring nature of the covenant with David and the certainty that it is as permanent as the heavenly bodies, which are free from the transitoriness of earthly affairs.

Part three, verses 38-52. The poet has sung the greatness of God and has reminded God of his covenant with the house of David. Now he depicts the actual state of the monarchy, the exact opposite of what God had sworn to his servant. The king has been totally defeated in war and is covered with shame. His cities are plundered and laid open, and it seems that all that was promised in the Royal Zion Festival has been repudiated. God is surely angry, for he has annulled the covenant he made with David and has smitten him with stripes more severe than mere human discipline could be. It is notable that even in the extreme of grief expressed here the Psalmist avoids saying that God has "profaned" his covenant. He has "profaned" David's crown, verse 39, but verse 34 contains the promise that he will never profane the covenant. In the greatest despair there remains trust in God's will.

The Psalm concludes with a powerful appeal to God, charged with emotion, to have pity on his servant, to show again the covenant love and the faithfulness that he long before had promised to David. Verse 52 is a doxology closing the third book of the Psalter, but it is also a fitting climax to this Psalm.

This Psalm, which must have been composed rather late in the history of the Southern Kingdom, perhaps toward the close of the seventh century B.C., illustrates the persistence of the royal ideology that undergirded the Davidic dynasty and shaped the life and thought of the people to so great an extent. In spite of the disaster that has overtaken the royal house, there is hope that it will yet be restored and that God's actions in history will be in accordance with his purpose which he announced centuries before. There is in this Psalm no explicit Messianic hope that transcends the historical scene, but the dynamic is there to aid in the development of that hope. More than that, the faith in God's promises in the midst of suffering helped prepare the people for the even greater disaster that lay before them, the destruction of Jerusalem and the end of the monarchy in 587 B.C. This Psalm clearly shows that the royal ideology had enough vitality to maintain its hold on the people even when the visible tokens of that ideology were swept away.

Psalm 101

A GUIDE FOR RULERS

1. I will sing of steadfast love and justice;
   To thee, O Yahweh, I sing aloud.
2. I will deal wisely in the way of uprightness;
   When wilt thou come unto me?
   I walk in the purity of my heart
   In the midst of my house.
3. I will not put before my eyes
   An unworthy deed.
   I hate him that doeth lies;
   He shall not cleave to me.
4. Let a perverse heart turn away from me;
   I will not know evil.
5. He who slanders his neighbor in secret,
   Him will I destroy.
   A man of proud eyes and a haughty heart
   I cannot abide.
6. My eyes are on the faithful in the land,
   That they may live with me.
   The one who walks in the right way,
   He shall serve me.
7. No one shall live in the midst of my house
   Who practices deceit.
   He who speaks lies shall not stand
   Before my eyes.
8. Every morning I destroy
   All the wicked of the earth,
   To cut off from the city of Yahweh
   All the evildoers.

The subject of the Psalm possesses a large house, verses 2, 7; it is a great honor to be chosen for his service, verse 6; he pos-

sesses great power, verses 5-6; and he has the judicial authority
to cleanse the city of Yahweh of all the wicked, verse 8. All
these factors point to the king as the one speaking in this Psalm.
Luther very aptly called it the *Regentenspiegel,* a mirror for
princes.[1]

This Psalm is outstanding in its moral earnestness. The king
acts as Yahweh's representative in judging the people in accordance with the divine covenant love and justice which are
prominently placed at the beginning of the Psalm. Psalm 72:1
indicates this divine commission given to the king, and the
following verses tell of the spirit in which it is carried out. Moreover, as king in Jerusalem, the ruler had a responsibility toward
the Temple, the center of the national worship—a responsibility
that all too many kings failed to carry out. He accepts the great
moral demands Yahweh makes on him, 2-4, before he stands
in judgment on the people, for his whole heart and life must be
blameless if he is to rule well. The generality of the terms em-
ployed is an indication not of vagueness but of comprehensive-
ness. Moreover, in verses 5-8, it is seen that the people stand
under the same code as the king. The wrongs that are con-
demned are entirely social rather than cultic; slander, pride,
deceit, lying, undermine the mutual confidence between ruler
and people and between a man and his neighbor. By contrast,
the faithful man, the one who walks in the right way, is favored
by the king and given preferment. The cleansing of the city,
verse 8, may have been a feature of the ceremonial of the festival
of kingship. In that case, no exaggeration is involved in the language used here.

In verse 3, the word translated "lies" (A.S.V. has "the work of
them that turn aside") occurs only here in Scripture and its
meaning remains uncertain.

Setting forth as it does the ideal conduct of the monarch,
the Psalm reflects not so much the actual conditions of the time
as the ethical standards inherent in the concept of kingship of
the Davidic covenant. It can therefore probably best be placed
in the ceremonial of the Royal Zion Festival as the reigning

[1] Schmidt, *Die Psalmen,* p. 183.

king's statement of loyalty to the ethical demands of his office. (A similar avowal of righteousness is found in Psalm 18:20-27.) Its solemn character is well suited to the earnestness of the festival. John the Baptist took the view of Christ's work in his proclamation as recorded in Luke 3:16-17 that is similar to many features of this Psalm, and the exalted Christ in the New Testament is judge of his chosen people (Acts 5:1ff.; Revelation 1:16; 2:1ff.).

Psalm 110

KING AND PRIEST

1. Oracle of Yahweh to my Lord,
   "Sit at my right hand
   Until I make thy foes
   A stool for thy feet."
2. May Yahweh stretch out from Zion
   The scepter of thy strength
   Rule in the midst of thy foes!
3. With thee are nobles in the day of thy army.
   In the glory of holiness, from the womb of dawn,
   Thine is the dew of thy childhood.
4. Yahweh hath sworn and will not rue it,
   "Thou art priest for ever
   After the order of Melchisedek."
5. The Lord at thy right hand
   Breaks kings in pieces in the day of his wrath.
6. He will judge among the nations,
   Filled with corpses.
   He smites heads over a wide land.
7. From the brook in the way he drinks,
   Therefore he lifts up his head.

Probably no other Psalm has suffered more at the hands of emendators and commentators than has this one, and there is still very little agreement as to its interpretation. Because the proposed emendations are conflicting and uncertain, the above translation is an attempt to translate the Hebrew text as it now stands. To take an example of a proposed emendation, Oesterley accepted one of the most interesting, originally proposed by Gunkel, in which he rewrote verse 3 to read as follows:

> In the day of thy birth thou wast honoured,
> Sanctified from the womb;
> From the dawn cometh forth the dew of thy youth.[1]

The translation of Leslie is very much like this,[2] and similar emendations are proposed for the rest of the Psalm.

The part of discretion is to admit the extreme difficulty of the text and try to translate it and interpret it as it now stands. The Psalm is probably a unit and should be treated as such in any interpretation. But may it not originally have been a part of a ceremony in which other hymns and ritual actions completed the message of this Psalm and made it clear? It would be hazardous to attempt to determine in detail its setting in Israelite worship or to use it as the program of any festival, but the features of royal ideology indicate a connection with the Royal Zion Festival even though this connection cannot be specifically defined.

Part one, verses 1-3, contains a divine oracle announced to the Davidic king, perhaps to David himself, by the prophet who received the oracle. The king is commanded to sit at Yahweh's right hand, the place of honor, in anticipation of the victory in which Yahweh himself will bring the enemies of the king into subjection, signified by the ancient concept of the victorious ruler's placing his foot on the neck of those he has conquered. It was in this way that Joshua and the Israelite elders emphasized their victory over the five southern kings, Joshua 10:24. This verse particularly emphasizes the fact that the Davidic throne is established by divine authority. In verse 2, the style changes from the oracular to the prophetic with an expression similar in meaning to the foregoing. God stretches out the royal scepter from Zion; that is, God gives the king the power to rule from the city he has chosen as his own dwelling. Compare Psalm 132:13-14. This is followed by the exhortation to the king to reign over his foes. Verse 3 is full of difficulties, as was seen by the nature of the emendations proposed. Indeed, aside from

---

[1] Oesterley, The Psalms, p. 462.
[2] Leslie, The Psalms, p. 101.

the concept that the royal army is ready and eager to fight, little is certain. The expression "womb of the dawn" may be compared with Isaiah 14:12, "Day-star, son of Dawn," with the implication that here are preserved echoes of an ancient myth of a goddess "Dawn." It is likely that in Israel this became a conventional expression, and little, if any, thought was given to its original meaning.

Part two, verses 4-7. Verse 4 gives the second divine oracle, this one introduced as a solemn oath which Yahweh has sworn and which he will not alter. The one receiving the oracle is constituted a priest forever, after the order of Melchisedek. This bristles with problems. First, if the king is addressed here, he is being invested with priestly authority, and there is no indication of such an investiture in the historical books of the Old Testament. Moreover, what is the significance of Melchisedek, who is mentioned in the Old Testament only here and in Genesis 14:18-20? In the Genesis passage he is the king of Salem (Jerusalem?) and priest of El Elyon, thus combining the royal and priestly offices. H. H. Rowley has proposed an ingenious explanation of this Psalm in terms of Genesis 14:18-20 and the obvious connection between the two passages.[3] In his view, Zadok was the Jebusite priest in Jerusalem before David conquered the city, and it was to the ancient temple over which Zadok presided that David brought the Ark of the Covenant (2 Samuel 6:17). In order to give legitimacy to the priesthood of Zadok, the historical account of the meeting between Abraham and Zadok's remote ancestor Melchisedek was circulated. The first three verses of the Psalm could then be interpreted as addressed by Zadok to the king, confirming him as king of Jerusalem, and the fourth verse as addressed by the king to Zadok, confirming the latter in his priestly office.

This is a tempting solution for it does away with the difficulty of trying to explain the priesthood of David, and at the same time gives a reasonable connection between Psalm 110 and Genesis 14. There are, however, difficulties. Rowley's interpreta-

[3] H. H. Rowley, "Melchisedek and Zadok" in *Festschrift Alfred Bertholet zum 80. Geburtstag*, pp. 461-472. Tübingen: J. C. B. Mohr, 1950.

tion involves reading "King of Salem" in Genesis 14:18 as "Malchishalem," a name equivalent to Melchisedek, and not a title at all, thus denying any royal office to Melchisedek. It would have been dangerous for David to bestow the priestly office on one who was descended from a long line of priests *and* kings as he might get the idea that he had a right to the royal office as well! Besides, there is no evidence that Zadok was the preconquest Jebusite priest in Jerusalem or that David made use of Jebusite shrines and cult personnel, with the possible exception of the spring of Gihon. At best, Rowley's careful reconstruction is highly conjectural.

There is no compelling reason for abandoning the traditional view that both parts of the Psalm are addressed to the Davidic king. Melchisedek was not only the distant ancestor of the Jebusite kings, who, by the way, had evidently ceased to reign by the time David captured Jerusalem, but he was also a revered figure in the traditions of the patriarchs. It was certainly fitting that David as king of the Israelite nation ruling in the royal city of the ancient priest-king should be considered as successor to one who, like David, brought those two traditions together. It has already been pointed out in Chapter IV that the king exercised priestly functions on occasion.

The second oracle, like the first, passes over into a prophetic style. Here God is called "Lord" just as the king was in verse 1. Moreover, God is seen as both judge and mighty warrior (cf. Psalm 24:7-10; Psalm 46:6, 8-10; Psalm 18:39ff.). He is always near the king to help him in war, and in particular when the great day of God's wrath comes. In that day God will judge the nations and smite his foes until the land is filled with corpses. The power involved in the victories of the king is not his own limited human power but the almighty power of God himself. This lifts the whole Psalm into the realm of the eschatological, looking toward God's final and complete victory over his foes. There are various parallels here to Psalm 2. The kings of verse 5 are parallel to the kings of the earth in Psalm 2:2, and "in the day of his wrath" to "then will he speak to them in his wrath" (Psalm 2:5a).

The concluding verse of the Psalm is cryptic, and it is possible that there was originally an additional section that has been lost. The subject of the line is the king, who drinks from a holy spring and as a result is refreshed. This may be a reference to the spring of Gihon where Solomon was anointed king (1 Kings 1:38-39) and which probably was considered as sacred in pre-Israelite times.

Of the Royal Psalms, this one found the most extensive use in the New Testament as a Messianic Psalm. In the Gospels it is recorded that Jesus quoted verse 1 as written by David and referring to the Messiah. If the Messiah is the son of David, how can David call him Lord? (Matthew 22:41-45; Mark 12:35-37; Luke 20:41-44.) Then in Matthew 26:64 Jesus brought the first verse of this Psalm into connection with the Son of Man in Daniel 7:13, and in this sense the verse was widely used in the New Testament, Romans 8:34; Ephesians 1:20; Hebrews 1:13; 8:1; 10:12; 1 Peter 3:22. In addition the specific theme of conquering the enemies of the king is cited in Acts 2:35; 1 Corinthians 15:25; Hebrews 1:13; 10:13. In the Epistle to the Hebrews, verse 4 was interpreted as referring to Christ, who had become a priest after the order of Melchisedek (Hebrews 5:6). This concept formed the basis of an extended section of the Epistle, chapters 5-7.

Psalm 144

THE ROYAL WELFARE

1. Blessed be Yahweh, my Rock,
   Who teaches my hands to war,
   My fingers to fight.
2. My Graciousness, and my Refuge,
   My Retreat and my Deliverer.
   My Shield in whom I trust,
   The one who subdues my people[1] under me.
3. O Yahweh, what is man that thou takest account of
      him?
   The son of man that thou thinkest of him?
4. Man is like a breath;
   His days like a passing shadow.
5. O Yahweh, incline thy heavens and come down;
   Smite the hills that they smoke.
6. Flash thy lightnings and scatter them;
   Send thy arrows and terrify them.
7. Send thy hand from on high;
   Rescue me and deliver me from great waters,
   From the hand of the sons of foreigners,
8. Whose mouth speaks deceit,
   And whose right hand is one of falsehood.
9. O God, I will sing a new song unto thee;
   On a harp of ten strings I will praise thee.
10. Who givest salvation to kings,
    Who deliverest David his servant.
(11) From the evil sword 11. deliver me,[2]
    And rescue me from the hand of foreigners.

[1] Compare Psalm 18:47.
[2] The traditional verse division is in the wrong place. This line and the
next three may be a textual variant to verses 7-8.

118

Whose mouth speaks deceit,
And whose right hand is one of falsehood.

12. Happy[3] our sons, who are like plants
   Growing up in their youth,
   Our daughters like columns
   Carved for the likeness of a palace.

13. Our garners are full, providing food in abundance.
   Our sheep bring forth thousands,
   And ten thousands in our lanes.

14. Our cattle bear,
   And there is no breach and casting forth,
   And no crying out in our streets.

15. Happy is the people with whom it is thus!
   Happy the people whose God is Yahweh!

The similarity of much of this Psalm to other parts of the Psalter, particularly to Psalm 18, has led some commentators to regard it as a late imitation of older forms and to divide it into two independent parts, verses 1-11 and verses 12-15.[4] Weiser's explanation of its peculiar character is that it was the product of a well-defined liturgical tradition which included the various poetical elements related to the ideology of kingship and that this tradition was subject to certain modifications in the course of its use in worship.[5] In this view, it is possible to regard the Psalm as a unit and to take it on its own merits.

The Psalm opens on a note of praise to God, who inspires confidence in himself and who equips the king for waging war. The resemblance to Psalm 18, particularly verses 2, 35, 47, and 48, is striking. The next two verses give expression, in traditional liturgical language, to the frailty of man and his insignificance except as an object of divine condescension (cf. Psalm 8:4). In this way, the scene is made ready for the petition for the theophany, verses 5-6; human pride has been eliminated and the contrast between God and man made vivid. The purpose of

---

[3] Conjecture. Hebrew reads "which."
[4] Oesterley, *The Psalms,* p. 569; Leslie, *The Psalms,* pp. 279, 430.
[5] Weiser, *Die Psalmen,* p. 550.

the appearance of God is the defeat of the king's enemies, verses 7-8, and in the full assurance that his prayer will be heard, the king raises his voice to God in praise for the salvation to be granted to the house of David, verses 9-10.

The blessing of God on the people is intimately related to the prosperity and welfare of the king. Since this is particularly true in the form taken by the cult, the latter part of the Psalm is to be regarded as an integral part of this liturgy. Foremost in the minds of the people is the well-being of their sons growing up into young men. The daughters are pictured as a graceful group of caryatids, columns of a palace carved in the form of maidens. And then the prosperity of the agricultural life of the people is set forth in terms of a flourishing rural economy. The people whose lot is blessed in this way is indeed happy, but greater than the material blessing is the incomparable blessing of knowing Yahweh as the only true God.

With its many similarities to the other lyrics of the Royal Zion Festival and the dual theme, prosperity of the king, prosperity of the people, this Psalm clearly belongs to the ritual celebrations of the Davidic kingship.

2 Samuel 23:1–7

THE LAST WORDS OF DAVID

1. And these are the last words of David:
   Oracle of David, son of Jesse,
   And the oracle of the man raised on high.
   The anointed one of the God of Jacob,
   The darling of the songs of Israel.
2. The Spirit of Yahweh speaks in me,
   And his word is on my tongue.
3. The God of Israel speaks,
   To me the Rock of Israel says,
   "The one ruling justly among men,
   The one ruling in the fear of God,
4. Is like the morning light when the sun rises,
   A morning without clouds.
   Through brightness after rain
   The grass (springs) from the earth."
5. For is not my house thus with God?
   For an eternal covenant he made for me,
   Ordered in all and secured.
   For all my salvation and all my delight[1]—
   Does he not make them spring forth?
6. And the base men, they are all as thorns thrust away,
   For men do not take them with hands.
7. But the man (who) smites them
   Arms himself with iron,
   And the staff of a spear.
   And with fire they are utterly burned up.[2]

[1] The *Biblia Hebraica* proposes the slight emendation followed in this line and the next.
[2] The word translated "in place" in the A.S.V. is probably a copyist's error from the following verse.

By the terseness of its style, this epigrammatic oracle has provoked many emendations, the more extreme of which amount to
almost total rewriting. The purpose of the exegete, however, is
not to demonstrate his own skill in writing Hebrew verse but
to explain the meaning of what the ancient poet wrote, insofar
as that is possible. The difficulty of the text is an indication of
the great age of this poem, and there is no convincing reason for
denying that it was written by David.

The poem falls into four parts of approximately equal length,
verses 1-3a, 3b-4, 5, and 6-7. The introduction, verses 1-3a, contains eight parallel lines. The word "oracle" is only rarely used
of the words of a man and it gives the lines a solemn character.
David characterizes himself in a variety of ways, the man who
was raised on high, God's anointed, the sweet singer of Israel
(or the darling of the songs of Israel). The word of God which
has now come to him through the divine Spirit has to do with
the nature of David's kingship and sets forth ideals for his suc-
cessors. This might be called the theological program for the
future of the dynasty. If the king will rule righteously and in
the fear of God, his reign will be prosperous like a land that is
blessed with rain and with the warm sun in a cloudless sky. The
agricultural prosperity of the land will be one of the results of
the king's good rule. This is in general the same thought expressed in Psalm 72:1-7 and 144:12-15.

Verse 5 has as its theme the Davidic covenant by which
David's house was established and made secure before God.
The connection with the Royal Psalms is clear, especially Psalms
2:7-9; 89:28-29, 34-37; and 132:11-12. The last stanza, verses 6-7,
draws the contrast between the righteous ruler and the wicked.
The general sense is clear even though the individual phrases
are somewhat obscure. The base man is compared to thorns that
are too sharp to be taken in one's hands but must be picked up
with an iron implement or spear with a long handle so that they
can safely be carried off and used for fuel. This stanza may be
compared with Psalm 101.

What is the relation of this little poem to the royal ideology
and to the Royal Psalms? It underlines the conviction that God

has chosen David and made an eternal covenant with him. David's house must rule justly and in the fear of God, and if it does so, then God's blessing will be poured out upon the people. The fate of the wicked stands as a warning to those kings who might deviate from the way laid out here. In short, this oracle agrees with and substantiates the view of the Davidic dynasty taken throughout this book, even though it is impossible to say how it may have been used in the cultic ceremonials of kingship.

Messianic Psalms

The Royal Psalms, as has been seen, are steeped in the ideology of the Davidic dynasty and presuppose the promises God made to David. In these various Psalms we see the recounting of the events surrounding the founding of the dynasty, Psalm 132, the royal ideology set forth at the beginning of the reign of a scion of David's house, Psalm 2, the moral principles on which the rule of the king is based, Psalms 72 and 101, the reconciling of the Davidic covenant with the covenant made at Sinai, Psalm 18, and an earnest plea to God to remember his covenant with David in a time when the fortunes of the nation were at low ebb, Psalm 89, as well as other related themes in the Psalms treated in the foregoing pages. Through all this there are two important questions for the Christian student of the Psalms, first the relation of these ancient hymns to the Messianic hope, and second the way the expectation of the fulfillment of God's promises in history gave way to an eschatological hope.

Psalm 89, with its persistent trust in God's covenant love in the midst of ruin and destruction, points the way to an answer to the second question. Out of the disappointments of history came a hope for the future. Most probably the turning point came in the days of Isaiah son of Amoz in the eighth century B.C., for it was then that the theological bases of the monarchy were seriously threatened. He began his ministry in the year that King Uzziah died (Isaiah 6:1) and to the young prophet God's having smitten the Davidic king with leprosy must have seemed to be a punishment more severe than "the rod of men" or "the stripes of the children of men" (2 Samuel 7:14). Then in the reign of Ahaz matters grew worse. Not only did Ahaz, the vassal of Yahweh, bound to Yahweh by both the Sinaitic and Davidic covenants, conclude an alliance with the king of Assyria (2 Kings 16:7-8) and become his vassal, but as an inevitable consequence he introduced the worship of the god Asshur into the very Temple of Yahweh in Jerusalem by putting aside the old brazen altar and setting in its place an altar copied from the one Tiglath-Pileser had in Damascus (2 Kings 16:10-14). The power of Yahweh was belittled, and the true God made in effect to appear to be the vassal of the god of Assyria. In such a time as that Isaiah proclaimed the power of God and the certainty that God would be true to his covenant with David and even yet place a righteous king on the throne of David in Jerusalem, the one whose name would be called, "Wonderful Counselor, Mighty God, Everlasting Father, Prince of Peace" (Isaiah 9:6, R.S.V.).

Later it was Isaiah's task to declare that God would protect the city of Jerusalem that he had chosen and not let it fall into the hands of Sennacherib (2 Kings 19:20-34). This became so embedded in the thinking of the Judeans that in the days of Jeremiah a century or so later they were certain that God would always defend his city whether the Davidic kings kept the demands of the covenant for justice or not. It took the devastation of the sack of Jerusalem and the deposition of the Davidic king to turn the hope of the people definitely into the future. The hope that had already been directed toward the future in the oracles of Isaiah now became clearly eschatological.

Where once the expectation that God would fulfill the promises he had made to David had centered around the new king coming to the throne in Jerusalem, it now was directed to the "Coming One" who would restore the house of David and reign in Jerusalem over the nations, ruling in righteousness and justice. There arose a longing for the restoration of kingship under a Messianic king, who would be essentially identical with the scion of David's line in the popular expectation of pre-exilic times, but who, unlike the monarchs of history, would truly fulfill God's promises.

There can be little doubt that the Royal Psalms served to keep this hope alive, although there is no way of establishing in detail how it was done. Even in view of their origin in the worship of pre-exilic times, the Psalms can still properly be called the hymn book of the Second Temple. In this period, the Royal Psalms, with their reminders of God's covenant with David and of the character of the reign of the coming king, surely played a leading role in keeping the expectation of the Messiah in the thoughts of the people.

This is the expectation which the members of the early church believed had been fulfilled in Jesus of Nazareth, whom they called the Christ, the anointed of the Lord. In the opening words of his letter to the Romans, Paul expressed this clearly. Jesus was "descended from David according to the flesh" and thus in the line that had received God's promises (Romans 1:3, R.S.V.). Moreover, he was "designated Son of God in power according to the Spirit of holiness by his resurrection from the dead" (Romans 1:4, R.S.V.). If this can be taken as parallel to Psalm 2, the Resurrection serves the same function as the coronation ceremony; that is, it proclaims the king as the Son of God. Obedience to his name is to be brought about among all the nations (Romans 1:5), just as in Psalm 2:8 the nations are to be his heritage. All this is the content of God's good news of victory promised of old through the prophets and now fulfilled (Romans 1:1-2). The ideal king of the Davidic line has come to fulfill the hopes that were attached to that line as a result of God's promises to David. To us is born "in the city of David a Savior, who is Christ the Lord" (Luke 2:11, R.S.V.).